My life is not heavy, it's delightful.
I live in a warehouse in the warehouse district of Redwood City, California.
I live with Bob, Sarah and Yossarian and a lot of tools.
I like computers.
I like to design betting and playing systems for blackjack.

If I were alone on a desert island and could only have 3 foods I would choose ice cream, oranges, and pizza pie.

                                                Jane Wood

Jane Wood

SELLING WHAT YOU MAKE

Penguin Books Inc.
Baltimore, Maryland

Penguin Books Inc.
7110 Ambassador Road
Baltimore, Maryland 21207, U.S.A.

Copyright © Jane Wood, 1973

Library of Congress Catalog Card Number: 72-94534

Printed in the United States of America

The line "They got a handful of gimme and a mouthfull of much obliged" on page 102 is taken from "Drop Down Mama" by Sleepy John Estes, Copyright © 1971 by Northern Music Company, A Division of MCA Entertainments Inc. Used By Permission. All Rights Reserved.

Dedicated to Simplicity

2 DIRECT SELLING 12

"Woodbridge Fuller and his big old dog stand around Fisherman's Wharf with a sign that says, 'Hug A Dog for 5¢.' Sometimes he gets enough huggers to make a few dollars. Once, by golly, business was so good people had to wait in line for a turn. Other times he waits for hours and wonders about the other places to be."

✷ SOME OTHER PLACES TO BE
✷ STREET SELLING ✷ ART
FAIRS ✷ SELLING ON CAMPUS
✷ SHOWS ✷ THE QUESTION
OF VALUE ✷ FINDING WHAT
PEOPLE LIKE ✷ PRICES ✷

3 LITTLE STORES 26

"Down in town there is the ultimate little store just tripping along on its own divine ordinariness."

✷ MARY LOU'S LITTLE STORE
✷ WHERE TO FIND THEM ✷ CON-
TACTING THE BUYER ✷ YOU ARE
THERE ✷ QUESTIONS MOST OFTEN
ASKED ✷ ABOUT THESE QUESTIONS
✷ LAST TRY ✷ YOUR MOMENTUM ✷

4 BIG STORES 50

"The buyer's office is a simple place where odd merchandise is scattered about, where an appointment book lies opened to a page with your name on it, where forms and memos make up the wallpaper and where Johanna is packing boxes on the side. Very unpresumptuous."

✳ THE DEPARTMENTS ✳ FINDING BIG STORES ✳ CONTACTING THE BUYER ✳ TIME AND PLACE ✳ YOU ARE THERE ✳

5 WHOLESALERS 68

"Wholesalers buy things, then sell them to little and big store buyers. It is very common for wholesalers to buy handcrafted work. Some wholesalers are stationary, some roam about and some do both."

✳ THE STATIONARY WHOLESALER ✳ THE WANDERING WHOLESALER ✳ PRICES ✳ TWO SITUATIONS - WHO TAKES THE RISK? ✳ A GRAPHIC SUMMARY OF SELLING ✳

6 PRESENTATION............78

"Patterns are needed in your display so a buyer can see the relationships in your work at the same time she is judging it, pricing it and thinking about calling her cat's vet during lunch break. You can make these patterns. That's what a presentation is all about."

✳ PRACTICALITY ✳ PATTERNS AND BALANCE ✳ BACKGROUND ✳ AN ORDERING SYSTEM ✳

7 FORMS & RECORD KEEPING.......90

"The best way to grok a form is to look at one head on. Once you have it in front of you, there is just the simple process of filling in the blanks."

✳ INVOICES ✳ PACKING SLIPS ✳ STATEMENTS ✳ TWO LEVELS OF RECORD KEEPING — SLASHING INVOICES & ACCOUNTS RECEIVABLE ✳ COLLECTING MONEY ✳ MINOR PROCRASTINATION OF THE PAYMENT ✳ CHRONIC PROCRASTINATION OF THE PAYMENT ✳

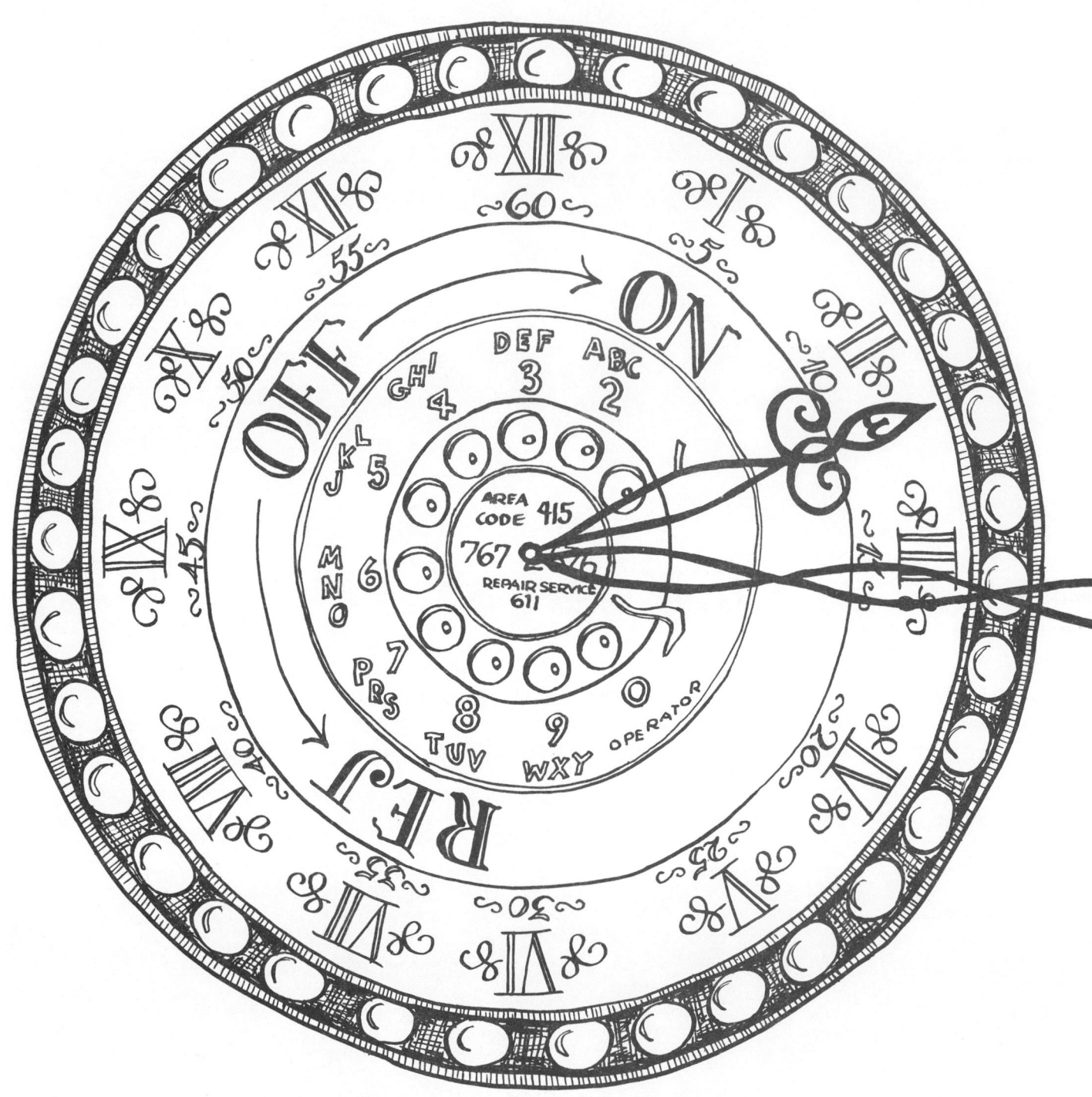

Have you ever made anything by hand and enjoyed it?

Have you given your friends something you made and now you want to make more?

Would you rather make things than get a job? Or did you already get a job, replacing the craft you do like with the security in the job you don't like now?

If any of these questions intrigue you, then this is your book. It will dilute the doubts that keep you from taking your work to a store and saying, "This is what I make. Want to buy some?..." It will dilute the doubts that make you ask instead, "What, me sell? I'm an artist, not a salesman." You don't have to be a salesman. In fact it's far better if you're not. I think selling for its own sake is complex and crazy. Selling what you make is simple and sane. I want to show you this simplicity.

OBSTACLES

Any obstacle to selling what you make can be traced to images. IMAGES are based on IMAGination rather than what is true. They are true only by accident. The hoax in images lies in their rigidity, like a picture in the mind that cannot move when everything else is changing, when you are changing, when your work is changing. Some images say, "Stay here!" Others say, "Don't go there!" They all eat up your motion.

STAY HERE images involve attachment. A person may <u>attach</u> himself to the image of the rambling street artist, or the home craftsman. Often a person linked with any part of these images may righteously give away his work or enjoy the idea that business is not in his personality. He may call himself gentle. He may see himself lacking a dynamite go-getter aggressiveness he thinks is necessary for selling. And he may say, "Oh, no! I cannot accept payment for my creations."

DON'T GO THERE images involve negative impressions. There is an image about the selling world - the crazy clock-timed unrhymed selling machine. Indeed the mechanical insanity is not a hallucination. Where the false image lies is in believing you must become mechanical. Selling does not make you crazy, images do. It's not what you do, but the way you do it.

These images are extraneous. They are directly opposed to your creativity, to your balance and to your being. Isolate what you have emotionally, intellectually and physically invested in an image, and there is just the easy part left - the part about diluting strangeness and unfamiliarity - the part where you remove the selling act from the dwelling chamber in your head where the minnows hang out (where the awareness of selling cannot be held or controlled) to a place where it's all quite easily grasped.

1
~ THE HILL ~

This hill expresses the space between rigidity and chaos. It shows where to channel your energy for seeking a balance in selling what you make. If you just "make" things you dwell on the west side of the hill. Your crafts mount up and your basement gets full. When you do not move what you have made... blah... no voids are formed. Creativity is squandered and you are in the desert.

WORKING AT HOME ~ DIRECT SELLING ~ SMALL

-RIGIDITY-

On the other side you can also move off the energy line by going too far. Mass-producing the same thing over and over inhibits change. You become a machine... clunk...clunk...and you will again sacrifice creativity.

STORES ~ BIG STORES ~ WHOLESALING ~ MASS PRODUCTION
-CHAOS-

W ← → E

THE PAST

But when your work has an OUTLET, a space can be made by each thing that is sold and gone away. Things move because you are more fluid... tra la la... and new designs flow into the voids left by past work.

There is magnetism at both sides of the hill; one side draws you to hold your work where you made it, rigid and marketless. The other side draws you to quantity production, chaotic and market-full. On one end you are held by the past; on the other you are lured by the future. Both ends are locked...

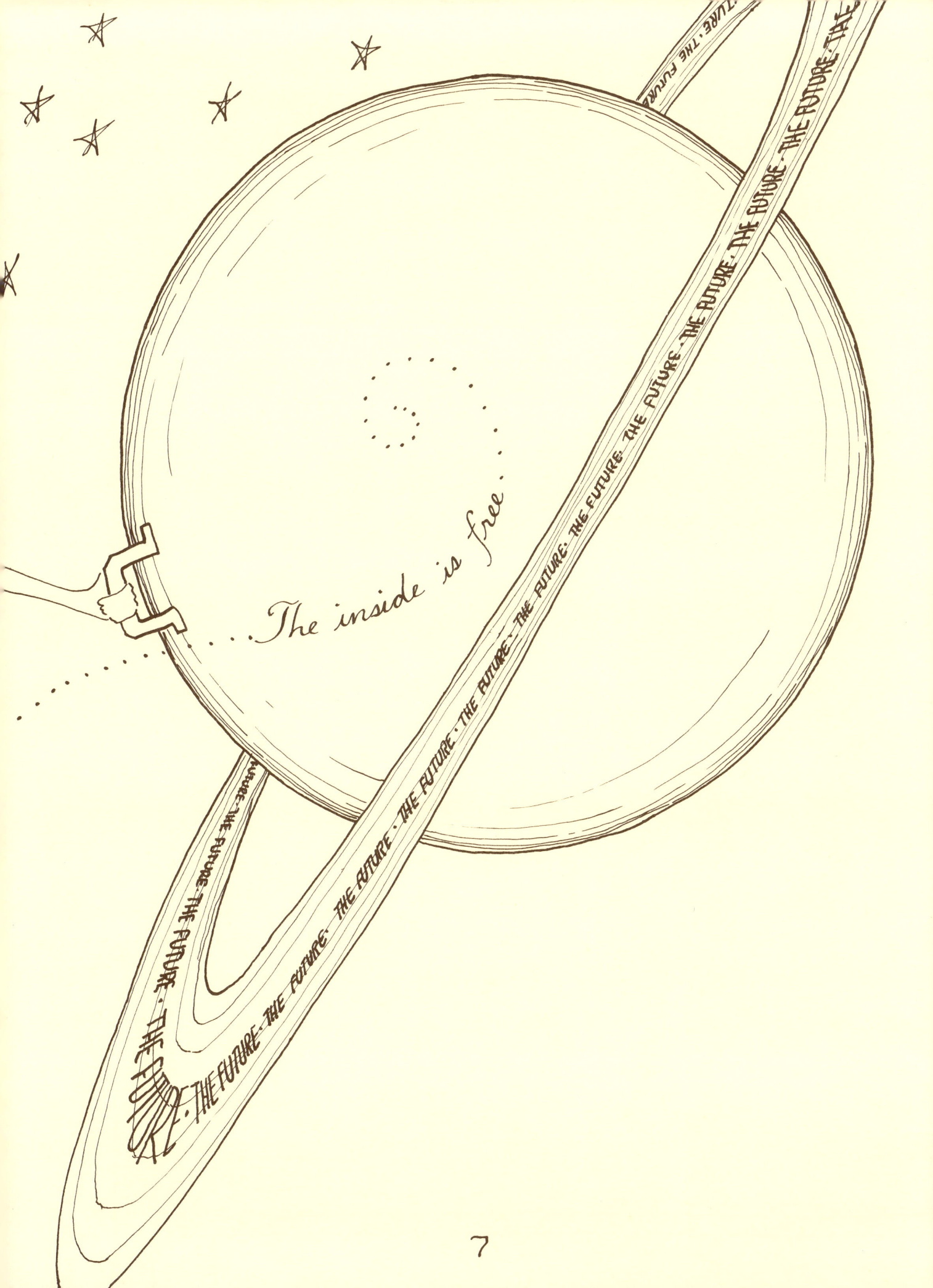

MOVEMENT →

Movement in any direction on the hill happens by doing different kinds of selling. In this process you will encounter

~ THREE VARIABLES ~

As you go east:
  1. the QUANTITY of what you sell increases,
  2. the PRICE you are paid per piece decreases.

Your place on the hill is not elusive. It is defined by the trip your product goes through before reaching the customer. This is the third variable:

  3. the number of STEPS between you and the customer increases.

HERE ARE THE STEPS:

Direct Selling
You..Customer

Little Stores
You........................Store Buyer.....Customer

Big Stores
You........................Store Buyer.....Customer

Wholesalers
You......Wholesaler.....Store Buyer.....Customer

Your product goes through these steps but you are involved with only one step. Nowhere on the energy line do you go beyond a person to person relationship. At small stores you deal with the store owner. At big stores you deal with buyers and in wholesaling you deal with the wholesaler — nothing complex, nothing heavier than selling a leather belt to a man passing by at an art fair. Outside the energy line relationships change. You encounter zero interaction on the side of rigidity where movement is not, and cluttered multi-interaction on the side of chaos where movement is artificial.

DIRECT SELLING

2

Woodbridge Fuller and his big old dog stand around Fisherman's Wharf with a sign that says, "Hug A Dog for 5¢." Sometimes he gets enough huggers to make a few dollars. Once, by golly, business was so good people had to wait in line for a turn. Other times he stands there for hours and at best sees a child who wants so much to touch his big beautiful mutt but whose parents pull quickly away. At times like these he wonders about the other places to be. All his thoughts come down to, "What am I doing here?" He is confronted with the QUESTION OF METHOD and the QUESTION OF VALUE.

THE QUESTION OF METHOD

Woodbridge is involved in direct selling ~ a one step method. A single movement happens between the maker and the taker. Street selling like this is one of many ways to reach the customer directly. Here are some others:

...SELL WHAT YOU MAKE...

Art fairs happen when a promoter gathers craftsmen and artists together to sell their work. They are held in shopping centers, inside dwellings, or on grassy hillsides. You can find out when and where the artfairs happen by talking to other craftsmen. Keep your eyes open for posters or look in local art magazines and newspapers. Some artfairs are fleeting in nature, happening one time only as a fund raising event. Others are established certainties called "circuits," given by one promoter in a different place every year or every weekend.

The average artfair lasts a couple of days. Booths are rarely supplied so bring something to display your work. A table may be all you need. You will be asked to pay two fees. One is the registration fee ~ usually under $10. The other is a commission between 10% and 30% of everything you sell. Sometimes a central cashier handles all the money transactions. Other times you handle all your own sales. Don't be afraid to accept checks. Bring lots of change so you won't have to run around trying to get change from the others who probably didn't bring enough either.

Some artfairs are discriminating. You might be asked to show samples or pictures of your work before you are accepted. This is good. It guarantees, to some extent, a fine environment to display what you make. You can't sell good quality work next to junk.

Once you have been part of an artfair you may find yourself on a mailing list that sends information about other artfairs. Make a mailing list for yourself too. Place a book by your display so people can write their names and addresses. Then next time you plan on being in an artfair, send notices to the people about when and where your work will be shown.

AT AN ART FAIR

"I WISH IT CAME IN RED!"

"QUITE EXPENSIVE!"

"A BIT TOO STRANGE!"

"IT'S UGLY!"

"WHOOPIE! I LOVE IT!"

"THE CURLY PART IS CUTE!"

"DO YOU MAKE BIG ONES?"

...OR ON A CAMPUS INSIDE A BUILDING...

Although there are often <u>written</u> laws about "soliciting in the dorms," they are balanced by <u>unwritten</u> curiosity and interest in handcrafted things. I have been selling this way for years to find what people like and what price range is comfortable.

The doors at the beginning or the end of the dorm halls are where the resident assistants most often dwell. Pass by these doors, as occasionally an assistant will disapprove of selling in the dorms. One time an extremely spaced girl jabbed her fingernails into my arm and dragged me down to some fancy place person regarding my selling. But even that turned out alright. The person asked why I had come and then purchased two pairs of earrings, saying, "Come back again tomorrow." The resident assistants' doors are labeled. And all the other doors are filled with fine curious people anxious for a quality diversion.

A good time to go is in the evening, Monday through Thursday, between 7:00 and 10:00. This is without a doubt the best time, as people are physically satiated from dinner and intellectually starved from the day. People at the dorms often want to postpone their payment or choice until a later date. I have found the best approach is to assume each time is the only time you will be there. If a person is going to buy something, he is just as likely to then as later. It is fine to accept checks, as the checks of dorm people are colorful and rarely of insufficient funds.

...OR OUTSIDE A BUILDING...

Selling on a campus~
Outside places can be found on many campuses that are good for selling what you make. The best times are Monday through Friday between 11:00 and 2:00 P.M. Go on a nice sunny day. Find the place that is the center of activity. Usually, it is toward the middle of the campus or near the student union. Sometimes these places are very green with lots of vegetation and people lying around. Sometimes they are quite exotic with fountains and sculptures or very high towers. The important thing is to be where people are moving without getting in the way by sitting in their path. Then all you have to do is sit there with your work and the people will come to you.

...OR GIVE A SHOW...

In essence, shows are self-organized artfairs. They are less common than other forms of direct selling because ordinarily they are given by people who do work in which each item is a separate entity~like sculptors or painters. Don't let this normality hinder you. Give a show for anything you like. Find a place to display your work, such as a local park, your house, somebody else's house or you could rent space in a building for a couple days. Then publicize your show by hanging posters around town. Send printed notices to people you know, or to people other people know, even to people nobody knows. Someone may have access to a mailing list that you can use. In time you will accumulate a good mailing list of your own.

When you set up the actual show try different ways to display your work. Make it **COLORFUL**. Decorate the place if you like. Do anything you like. Go crazy.

Shows are good to do with a group of people too. One craft compliments another and you will be able to see the niche your work fills in the whole created by all the crafts together.

THE QUESTION OF *VALUE**

At the last step of every selling process is a person — a customer — the one who finally drinks from your hand-thrown cup. The value of direct selling lies in the input you gather about this last person. You find how he feels about your work and how he feels about price. You will accumulate very useful impressions of your work through customers' eyes.

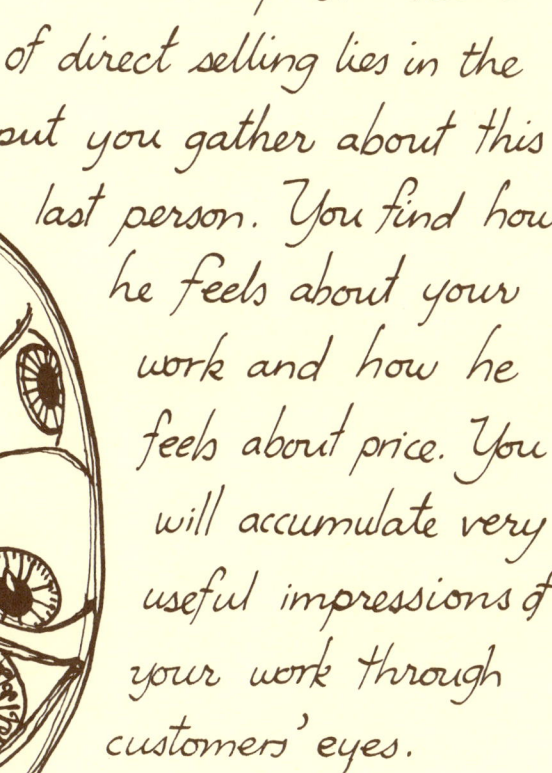

Some awareness of peoples' likes and dislikes comes from reactions of the people you know, like when your friend says, "Hey, I like this one... and that one is a little weird..." But there are other aspects of awareness that come best with real live direct selling. People feel one way about an object when they are just looking and another way when they are contemplating buying. Also, in direct selling you escape the HUMAN COLANDER.

The feeling a person has about YOU creates this sieve, through which his reactions to YOUR WORK are inevitably filtered. There is more objectivity in strangers.

Another value in direct selling is finding the right price. When setting a price there are two reality systems to consider ~ yours and the customer's. Yours is based on the material value of your work and your time. This basis is objective. The customer's reality system is based partly on his subjective idea of the material and time in your work and partly on how he imagines the thing you have made is going to look hanging on his wall or on his body or wherever it will finally be.

I have found in experimenting with prices that there is a lower limit below which a person may be hesitant to buy. If the price is too low he may think something is wrong, as if the thing will disintegrate when he gets it home. There is an upper limit too. But if someone expresses a feeling that your price is high, it does not necessarily mean you are above the comfort range. How often have you bought something you felt was expensive? As my friend David says about the prices he puts on his work, "No matter what amount I set, people say, 'It's a lot,' but they never say, 'It's too much.'"

Remember ~~ the value of direct selling lies beyond a balance of price or quantity. The value is in knowing what people want to buy. This objective knowledge is a link to all other kinds of selling to stores because unlike the final customer who wants what he likes, a store buyer wants what will sell. Any information you can give the buyer will be advantageous. The I Ching says, "Good fortune, how could this be a mistake?... The place is correct and central."

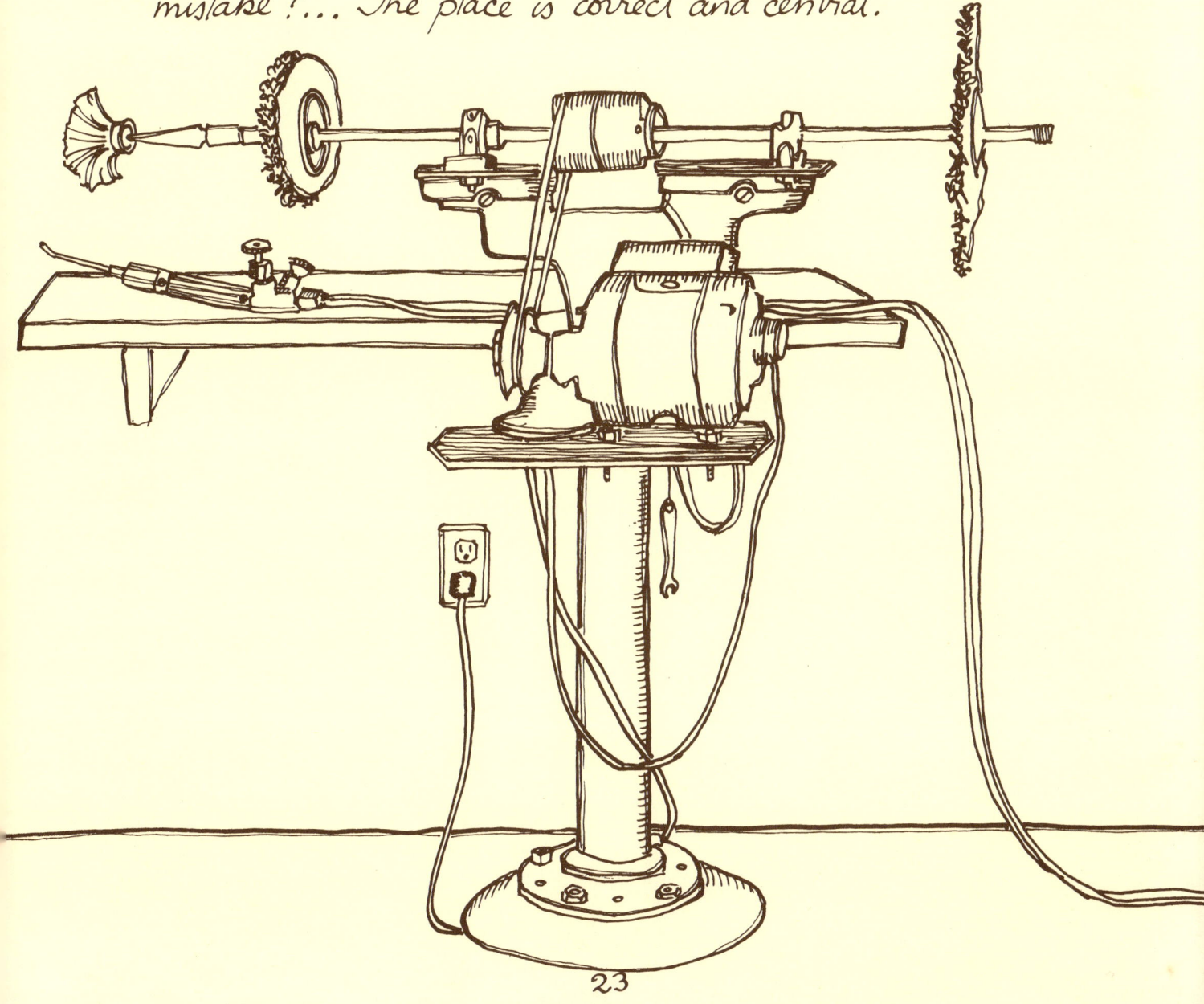

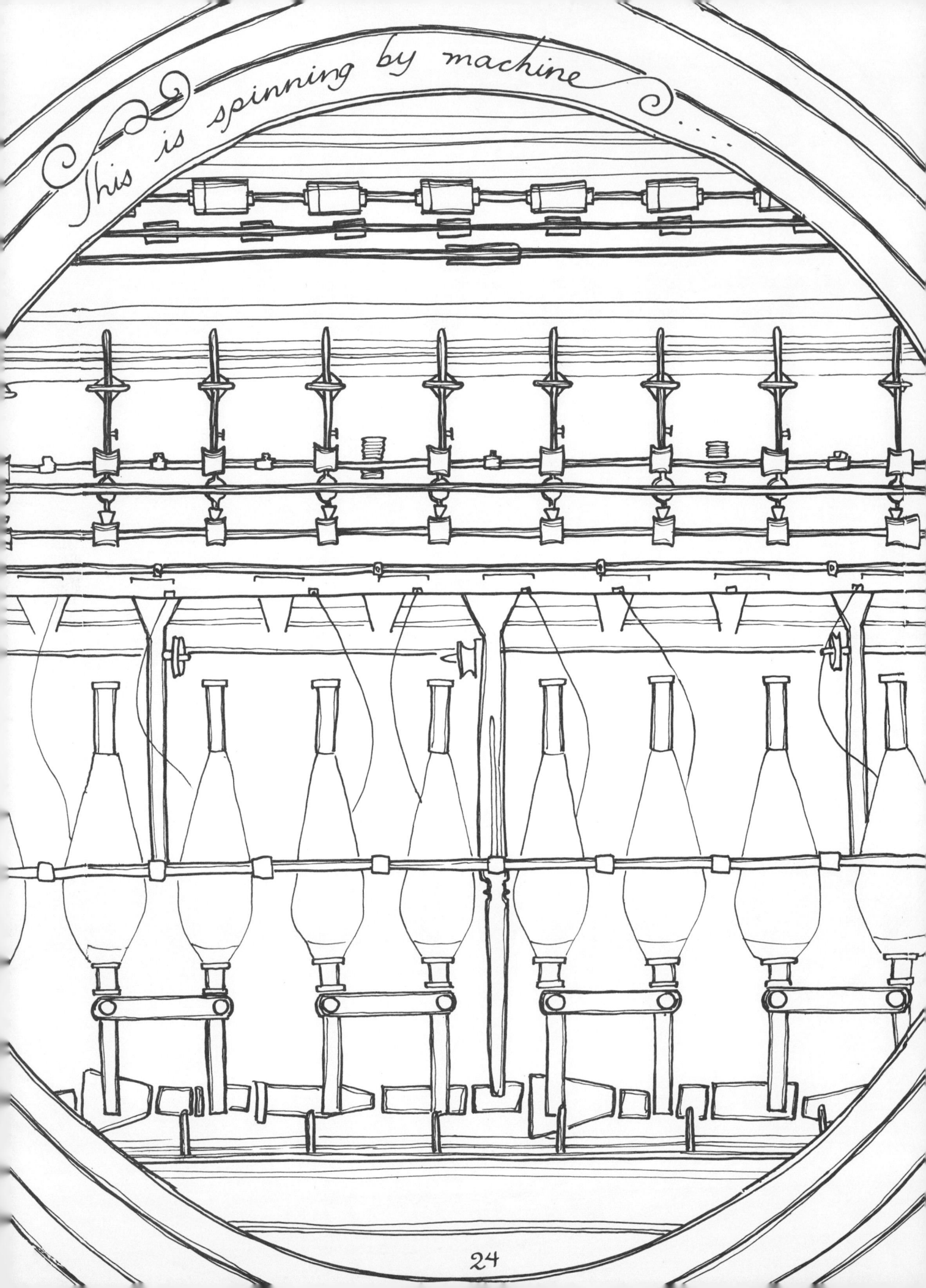

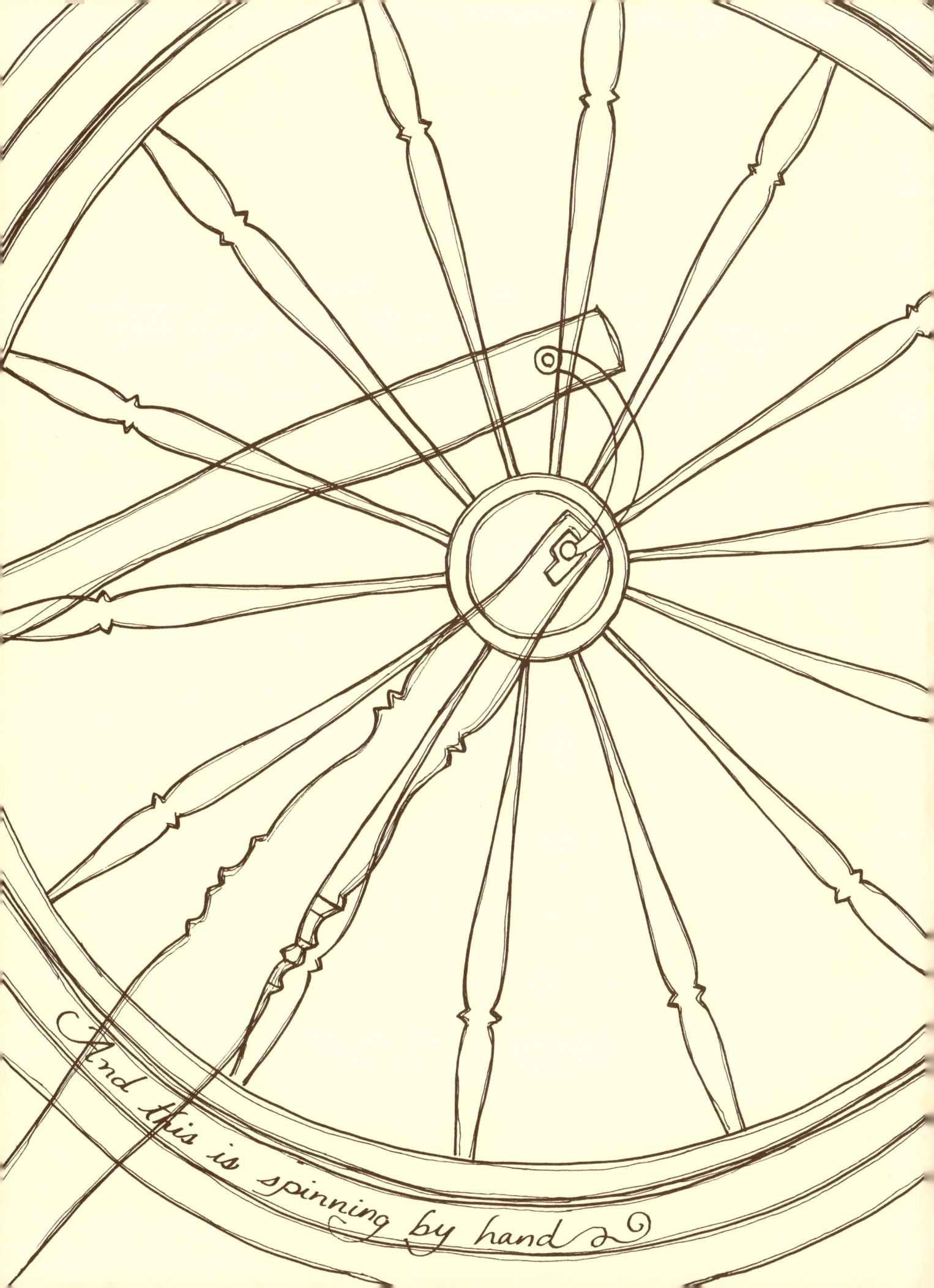

3
～ LITTLE STORES ～

Down in town there is
the ultimate little store just
tripping along on its own
divine ordinariness. Mary Lou
runs it, she'll show you around, she's
the cashier, the buyer and the bookkeeper.
When the light burns out, Mary Lou
fixes it, and she made the sign that's
hanging on the door.

The little store IS where your product
will be; nothing gets sent to the place
across town. This simplicity enables you
to be in and feel the environment in
which you are selling.

WHERE TO FIND LITTLE STORES
AND WHAT TO DO WHEN YOU DO ~

They are everywhere. They come in the form of boutiques, head shops, import stores, craft stores and gift shops. You see them all the time and when you do ~ note them and save all these store names and addresses. This RANDOM SEARCH is one way to come in contact with the market. Writing them down rather than trying to remember is important, as it avoids cluttering the space in your mind for creative work. Store names, peanut butter, and errands floating around in your head gather together in the receptacle of obligations, churn together and form potent globules of guilt, indeed a hindrance to your motion.

A second way to find stores is an INTENTIONAL SEARCH when you are in town. There are places where they are clustered, like Fisherman's Wharf or Sausalito. There is Read St. in Baltimore, Georgetown in D.C., Union St. in San Francisco and Cherry Creek North in Denver. In every city there is such a cluster. In every cluster there is a fantastic outlet for your craft.

You can find these stores in a third way by a WALK THROUGH THE YELLOW PAGES. The relation of your product to the atmosphere is not as accessible but you are less dependent on chance. Here is a list of headings from the San Francisco phone book. All phone books are pretty much alike. Some of these headings will seem absurd and on a closer look may make some sense. Others will seem quite related to your work and on a closer look become absurd . . . . .

Surrender yourself to the incredible

Yellow Pages

and extract your own relevance....

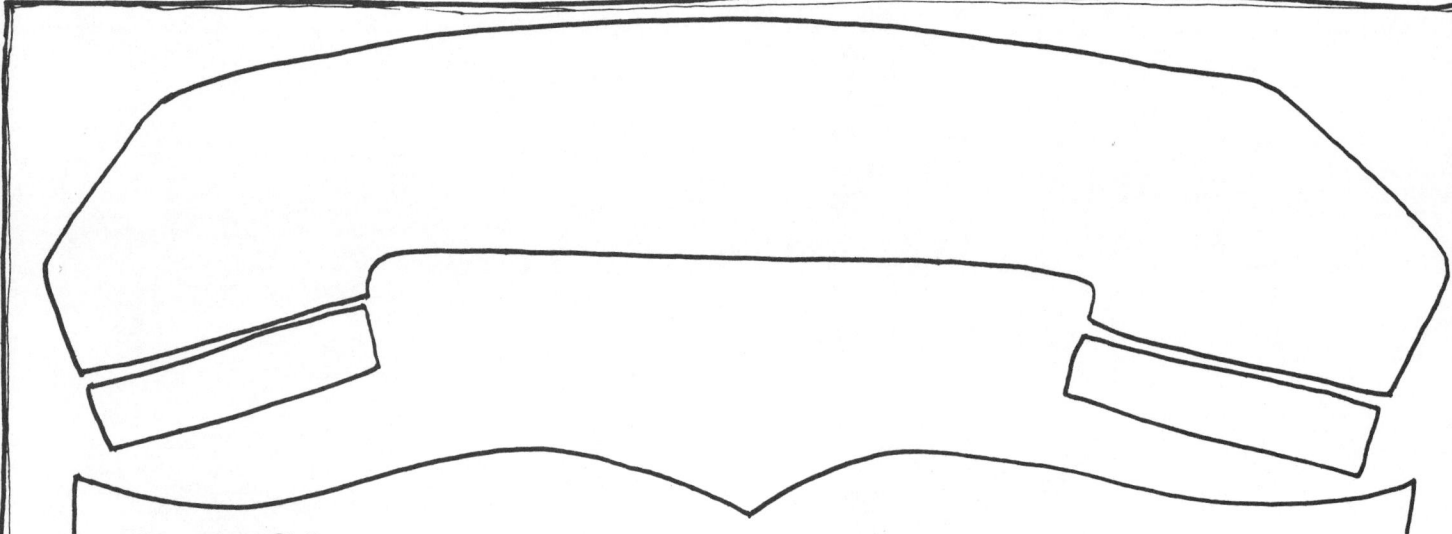

- BLOUSES
- BOUTIQUE ITEMS
- BOYS' CLOTHING
- CANDLES
- CERAMIC SPECIALTIES
- CHILDREN'S CLOTHES
- CHRISTMAS DECORATIONS
- CLAY PRODUCTS
- DESIGNER'S APPAREL
- DRESSES-RETAIL
- FURNITURE DEALERS-NEW
- GARDEN ORNAMENTS
- GIFT SHOPS
- HANDBAGS
- HOUSEWARES
- IMPORTERS
- JEWELERS
- LEATHER APPAREL
- MEN'S CLOTHING
- MOSAICS
- NECKWARE
- ORIENTAL GOODS
- PICTURES
- POTTERY
- SHIRTS
- SHOPPING CENTERS
- STATIONERS
- TOYS
- WOMEN'S ACCESSORIES
- WOMEN'S APPAREL

I should mention here that in any kind of search for stores the word "import" is frequently meaningless. Such stores do carry out-of-the-country goods but they have local items too. Not all those enchanting oriental-looking earrings were created in the magic of the East.

Another way to find stores is to talk to the people who work in the stores you have already found. Very likely they will know of some places that could be interested in your work. Also, you can find some in the advertising spheres of stores such as local newspapers, college newspapers and underground publications.

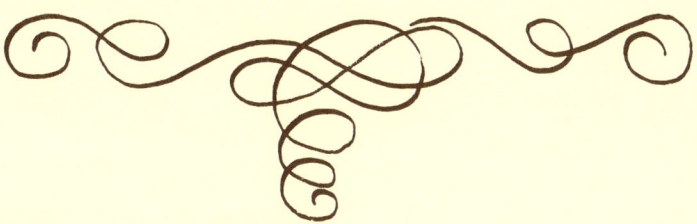

CONTACTING THE BUYER

You are now at a point where you can either call the buyer or drop in. From the standpoint of most buyers in small stores, it really doesn't matter which you do first. So figure out what is most convenient for you. When you find a CLUSTER of stores, it's probably best to stop in one after another, keeping track of which ones to revisit by writing information down or taking their cards. There is a generosity in card giving that will have your pockets bulging ~ pockets full of mumbles. If the buyer is not in, ask for his name, then you're even better off when you return. People like to be called by their names. It is a sane desire.

On the other hand, if you have a RANDOM COLLECTION of store names gathered from little notes, people, advertising, and the yellow pages, then it is best to use the telephone. Ask first to speak with the buyer of the store. Talking to others about your work wastes time and decomposes your momentum. So if the buyer is not there, ask for his name and when he can be reached.

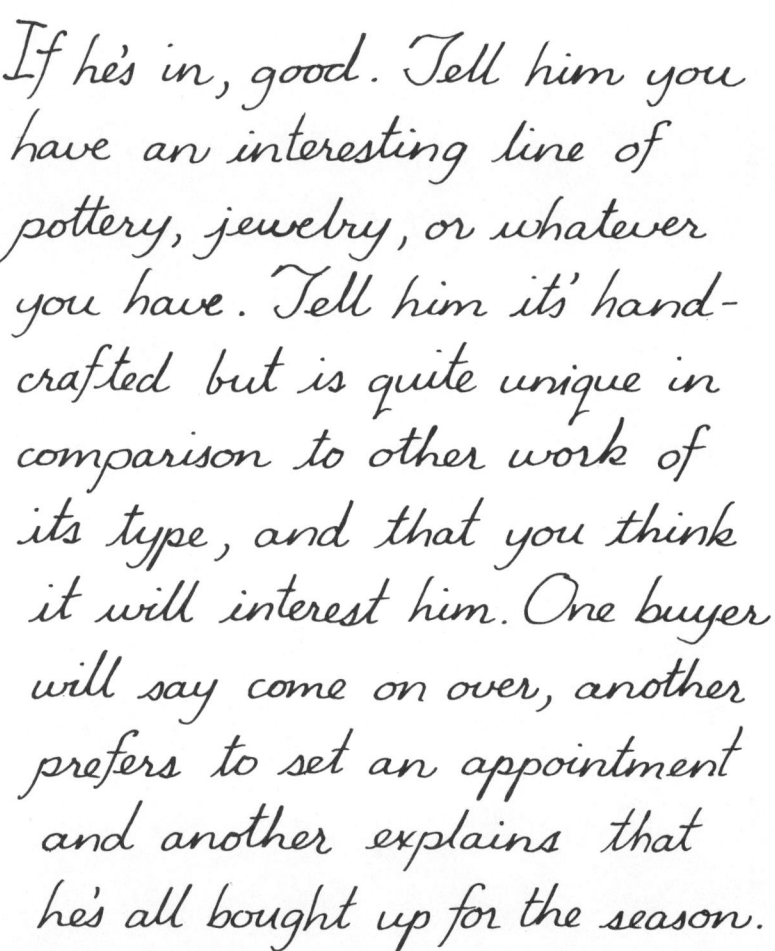

If he's in, good. Tell him you have an interesting line of pottery, jewelry, or whatever you have. Tell him it's hand-crafted but is quite unique in comparison to other work of its type, and that you think it will interest him. One buyer will say come on over, another prefers to set an appointment and another explains that he's all bought up for the season.

At this point ~ when the buyer does not have your work in front of him ~ don't try leading him into any commitments. A "yes" commitment can lead the buyer into false images about your work, which he hasn't even seen yet. And a "no" commitment places you at a disadvantage before you get there. So it is best for you to have the buyer decide about purchasing when the work is in front of him. Remember that your aim mingles not with selling but with getting there. This makes the situation clear and simple.

YOU ARE THERE ✸

Meeting with the store owner or buyer is like any other interaction on a normal day. It's like going to the vegetable store. Sometimes there's a little talk to begin with, like: "Did you have any trouble finding the place?.... Where are you from?...." Then to make room, ashtrays and things are moved off some space or sometimes you go to a little room in the back where other ashtrays and things are moved aside for your presentation. Then, "Let's see what you got." Some buyers sound hassled, others genuinely interested. Some give an apathetic grunt, others show wide-eyed pleasure. Each one is in a different place on the endless range of people-types. It is the same range in which you also have a place.

THE QUESTIONS
most often asked are these:

What is the price?
How did you make this?
Does someone help you with your work?
Can I buy these, or do I order?
When and how do you deliver?
Do you sell to any other stores?
What sells best?
May I take these on consignment?

ABOUT THE QUESTIONS:

What is the price?

The prices should be clear by your presentation in combination with a simple explanation. Quantity prices are good when you have lots of small things, like jewelry or little painted rocks, or when you have low-cost items. If a given piece is under $2.00 wholesale, for instance, then the price could be per dozen. Make your quotations consistent among stores. This is an unwritten rule based on emotions. If one buyer finds you have sold to another buyer at a lower price, he will probably FEEL that he got a rotten deal.

How did you make this?
For this interest in technique, sometimes photographs are good, depending on the craft. Explaining HOW you made it means showing your uniqueness. The process in your art can be part of what separates your work from the rest. More on presentation in Chapter 6.

Does someone help you with your work? Sometimes this question is asked to find if you are capable of filling large orders. Whether or not you do all the work yourself, it is good to make the buyer aware of what size order you are capable of filling.

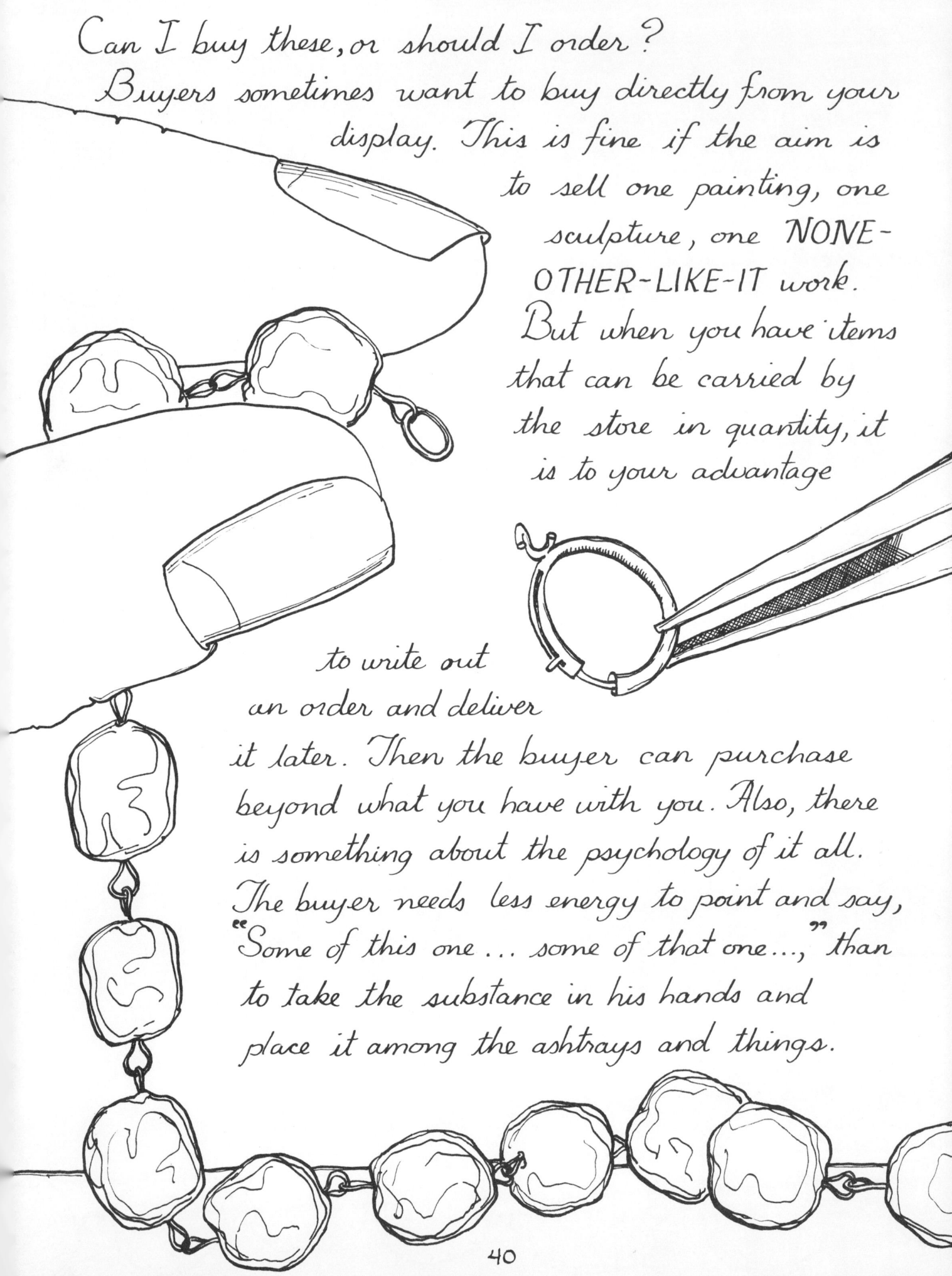

Can I buy these, or should I order?

Buyers sometimes want to buy directly from your display. This is fine if the aim is to sell one painting, one sculpture, one NONE-OTHER-LIKE-IT work. But when you have items that can be carried by the store in quantity, it is to your advantage to write out an order and deliver it later. Then the buyer can purchase beyond what you have with you. Also, there is something about the psychology of it all. The buyer needs less energy to point and say, "Some of this one... some of that one...," than to take the substance in his hands and place it among the ashtrays and things.

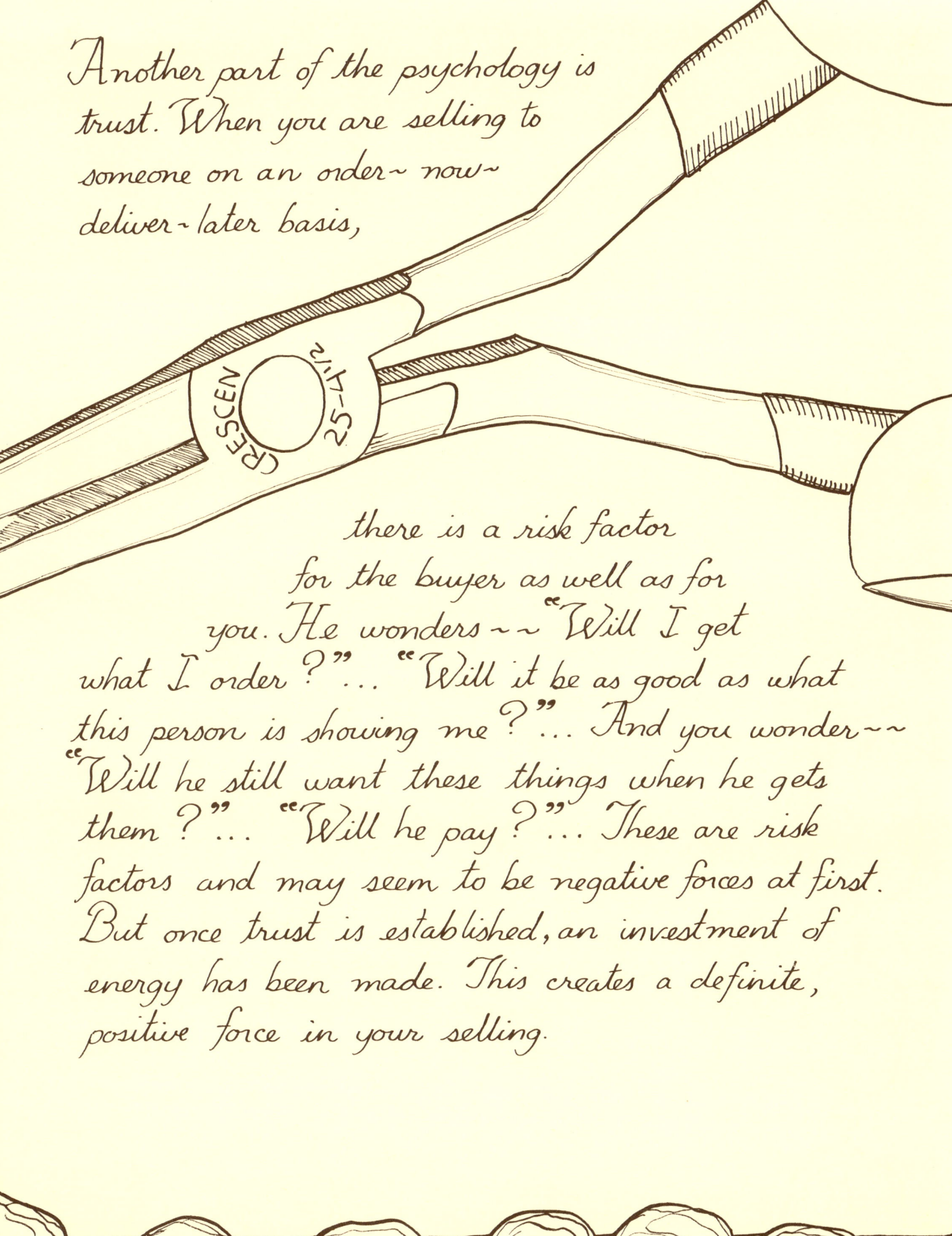

Another part of the psychology is trust. When you are selling to someone on an order~now~deliver~later basis, there is a risk factor for the buyer as well as for you. He wonders~~ "Will I get what I order?"... "Will it be as good as what this person is showing me?"... And you wonder~~ "Will he still want these things when he gets them?"... "Will he pay?"... These are risk factors and may seem to be negative forces at first. But once trust is established, an investment of energy has been made. This creates a definite, positive force in your selling.

When and how do you deliver?
A common delivery expectation is around 14 to 21 days but it varies depending on the craft. Be able to give a realistic estimate of the time it takes to make what you are selling. Then the delivery date can be decided between you and the buyer.

Concerning HOW to deliver: it might be easier to take the work to the store yourself if it is nearby. Or you can send it. If you charge the delivery costs to the store ~ which you can do ~ then the store expects you to send it the cheapest way ~ parcel post. Sometimes stores have special shipping instructions. More about this on p. 63.

Do you sell to any other stores?
This brings up the question of exclusives, which means having your work in only one store. At one end of the scale are stores which sell only exclusive items. At the other end are stores which never consider the idea. Most stores are somewhere in between, caring only if you are selling to the place next door or down the street.

You might get into a situation where you have an order from one store and nearby you find a second store that wants to sell your work exclusively in that area. The only thing you can do is be straight. Suggest to the second store that he could carry those parts of your work that the other place did not order. Or, if the second store seems a whole lot better for your work, then you could agree to the "exclusive" arrangement and explain to the first store that you have found a satisfactory outlet to handle the whole area.

What sells best?
Your opinion of what people like in your selection is valuable to the buyer. This opinion is the expression of all that you have gathered from selling direct to people, or from trends you have noticed in selling to other stores.

May I take these on consignment?
Consignment is when you leave your work in a store but collect no money until something sells. Then you receive somewhere between 50% and 80% of the retail value and the store takes the rest. The difference between consignment and buying is that the element of risk (of your work not selling) is shifted from the buyer to you. For accepting this risk you are paid more when your work does sell.

Two situations make the consignment question probable. One is the size of the store. Mary Lou, who runs the small store, is likely to request consignment. Some big place probably won't. The second situation is when a person is selling expensive items like sculpture or gold rings with precious stones. Other times consignment has no valid basis for you. The buyer may not be sure that your work will sell so he will see if he can try it out for free. That's a drag for you so tell him you sell only directly. Many times, when a buyer is denied consignment, he will end up buying the work anyway.

Last Try

For each reason a buyer does not want to take your work, you can make a corresponding last attempt to change his mind. When he says he has too much stock or that the money is low or that he's not sure it will sell, you can suggest making just a small order. When he says he cannot buy now but maybe later, you can say that you are establishing new accounts now but later will be involved in filling orders. That may not be true, but it is something you can say if you want to. If these immediate attempts don't work, even though the buyer is interested to some degree, then you can hang loose and come around again some other time.

Your Momentum

The process of creating a market does not always have consistency in its movement. Sometimes it's slow... doo dum dee doo... then it's **FAST**. You might spend several days visiting stores and they all seem to have no money, or they already bought what you are selling the day before you arrived. Even two days is a long time to go with scrawny results, let alone none at all. Momentum can be low because your motivation must come from somewhere outside yourself, especially in the beginning when so much significance is placed on each attempt. Remembering about unevenness in selling helps give you momentum so you can ride out the times of scrawny results.

FORTUNE.... WHICH BY FAR MAKES UP FOR THE SLOW DAYS.

If you have gone to several stores per day and find yourself in a lull for more than a week straight, then reassess your approach. It could be something simple. Try different ideas: experiment with prices, rearrange your display and the way you present it, think about trying other kinds of stores. The best way to find out what changes you might make is to ask the people in the stores what they think. They may have impressions you never considered. The simplest things in your work can make the difference between a lull and a run of accomplishment.

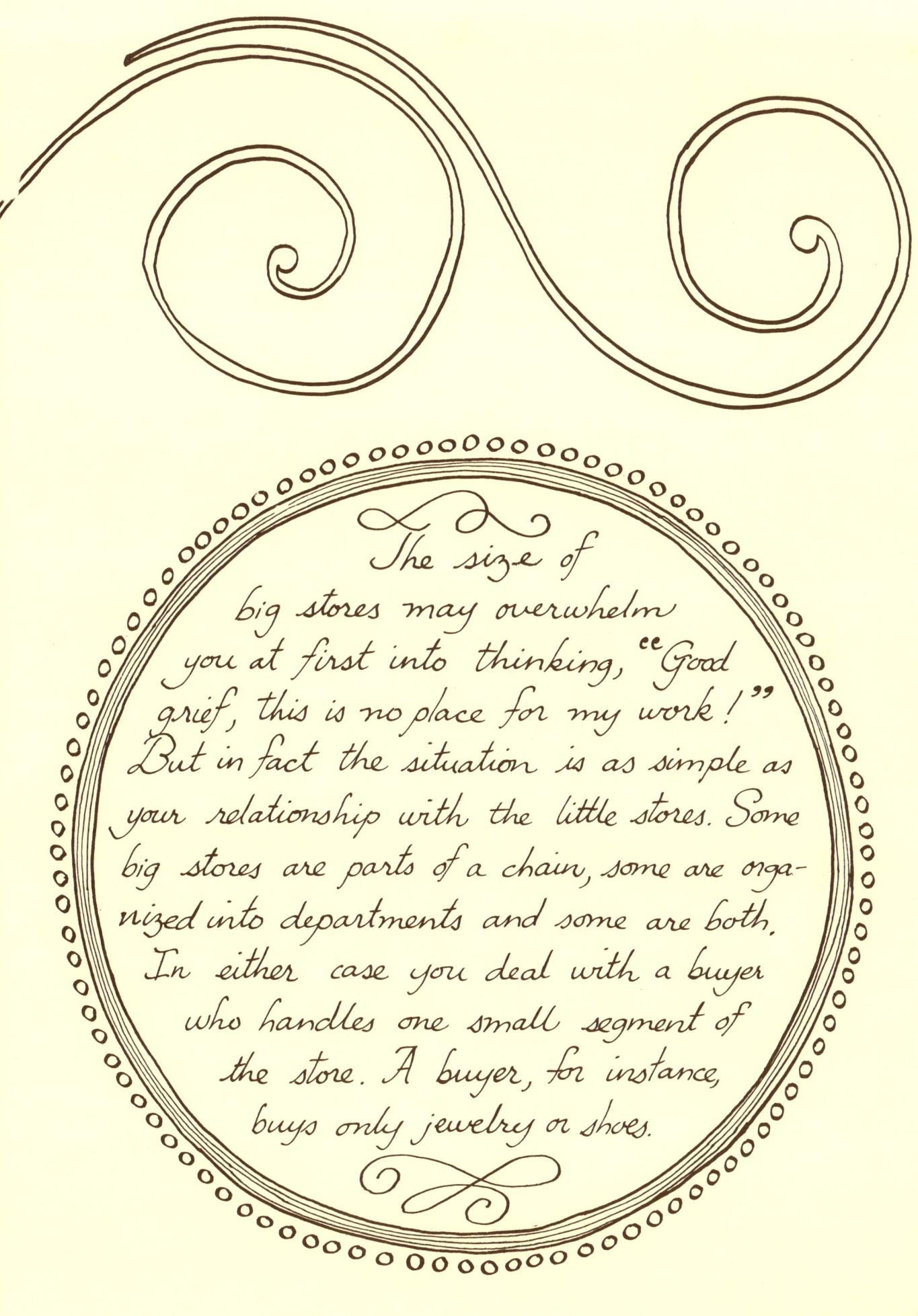

The size of big stores may overwhelm you at first into thinking, "Good grief, this is no place for my work!" But in fact the situation is as simple as your relationship with the little stores. Some big stores are parts of a chain, some are organized into departments and some are both. In either case you deal with a buyer who handles one small segment of the store. A buyer, for instance, buys only jewelry or shoes.

DEPARTMENTS

are the sections described by signs inside the store hanging from the ceiling and from the walls. Here is how a typical big store is divided ~

FIND YOUR NICHE:

COSMETICS STATIONERY
BOOKS RUGS
HOUSEWARES LADIES' WIGS
NECKWARE LINGERIE
FABRICS JEWELRY
BOYS' WEAR
SHOES ART & NEEDLEWORK
MENSWEAR GIFTS COATS
TOYS HOSIERY
LINENS NOTIONS
FURNITURE HANDBAGS ~
WOMENS' SPORTSWEAR

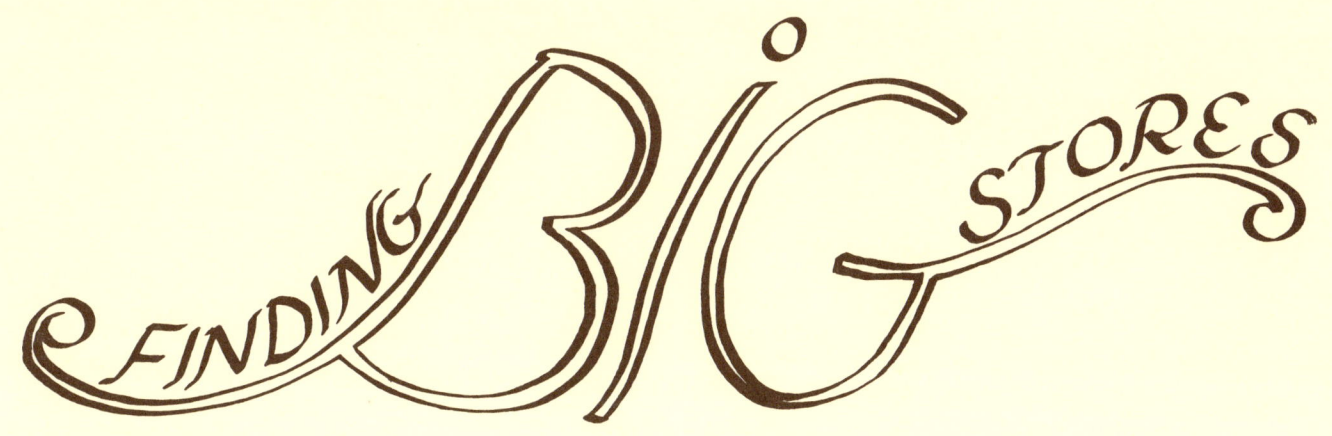

You can probably name a number of big stores even before you begin looking. They are a recurring entity among shopping centers, and even if you are not a shopping center-goer, the big-store signs are still visible -- flashing in the sky as you drive down megalopolis roads. If you are in an area new to you, then the yellow pages will again serve as a guide. Look under the heading called SHOPPING CENTERS.

Other big stores are harder to find and are often discovered by accident. You may suspect a place is one small simple store, quite apart from any self-repetitions, only to find it is one of a whole chain of others. This is a good find. Ask where you can locate the buyer.

Contacting the Buyer

The buyer's office is probably at one of three places: 1.) near her department at the main store, 2.) in a separate buyers' section at the main store or 3.) in a whole separate building just for offices, possibly an industrial park. Most of the time, however, the buyer is somewhere else in the store, or checking inventory at the warehouse, or off on a buying trip to New York City. So for your convenience and hers, it is best to use the telephone again.

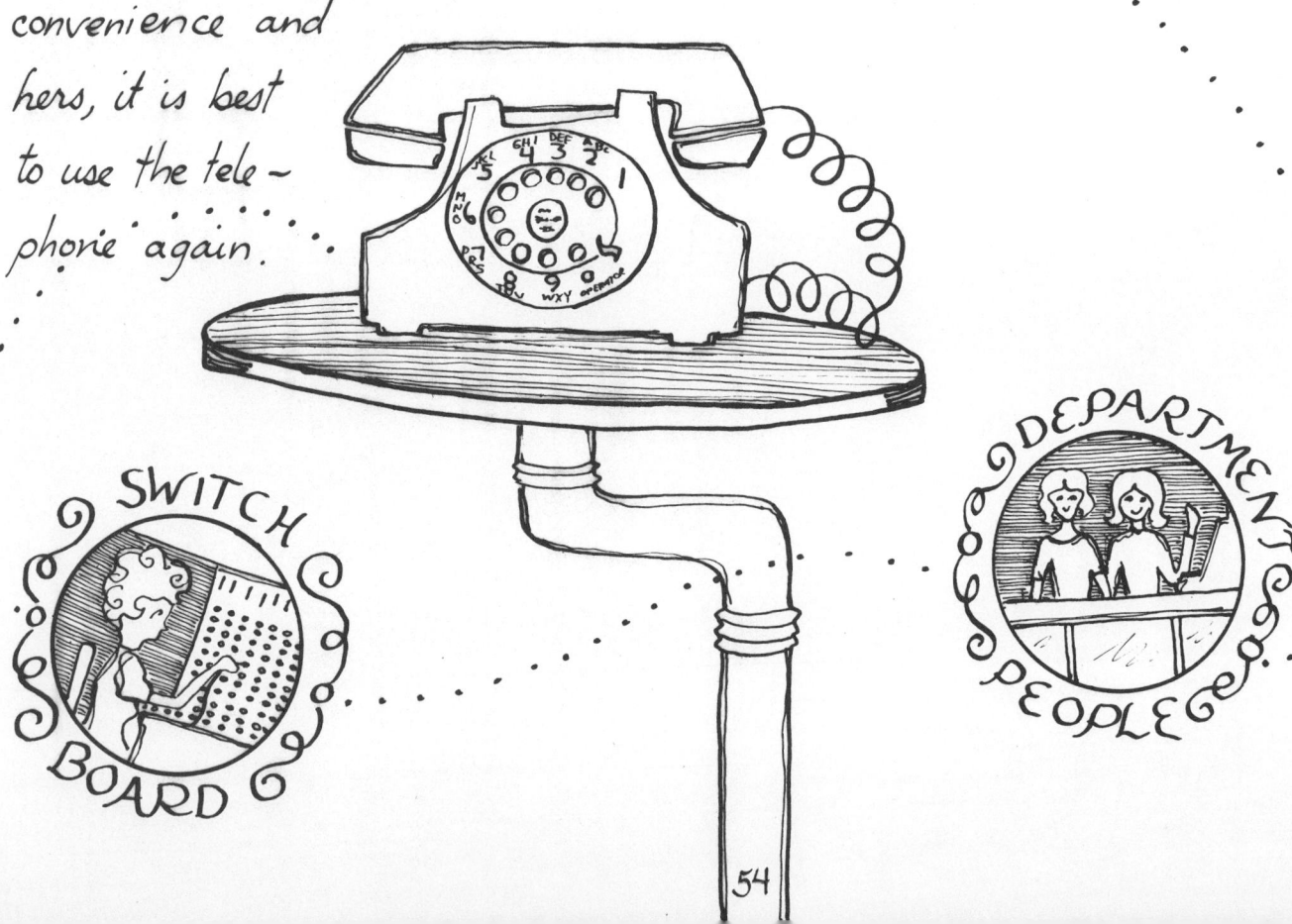

People at the Mis-Connections

When you call, do as before; speak only to the buyer. You may find yourself on the line with switchboard operators, people in the department, assistant buyers and people at the other end of the line when you get connected to the wrong place. These side trips are no problem when you confine your intentions to reaching the buyer. If you are calling long distance, do it person to person and assume that messages to return calls hit the trash can as soon as they are written.

The best TIME to meet the 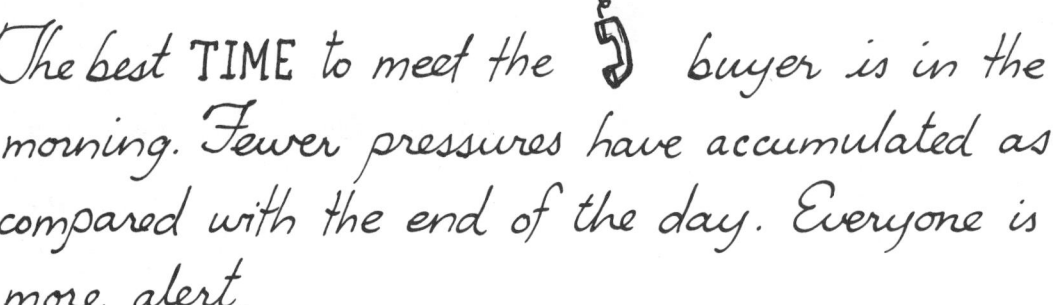 buyer is in the morning. Fewer pressures have accumulated as compared with the end of the day. Everyone is more alert.

The best PLACE to meet the buyer is in her office, which is usually her preference anyway. This is good for you because a person is more likely to fulfill the functions of a role in the surroundings of that role. So it makes sense that a buyer is more susceptible to buying in the security of her buying surroundings. Her inventory information and purchase orders are also there.

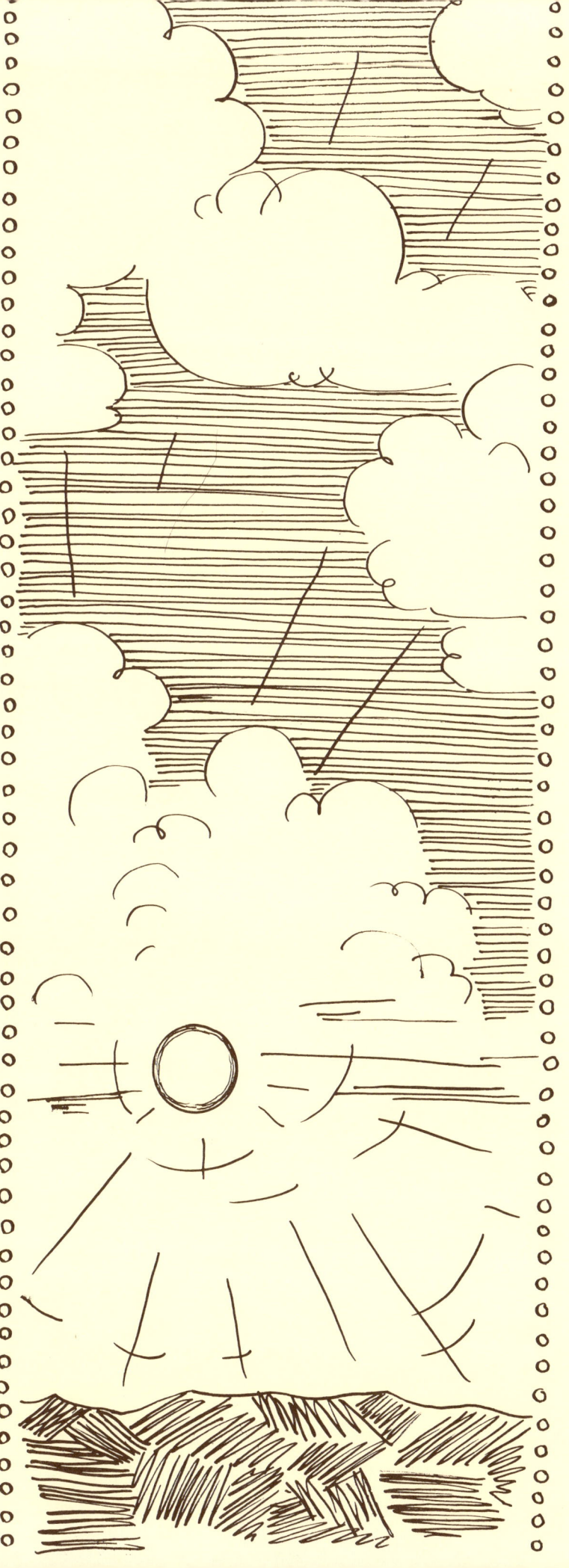

YOU ARE THERE.... EVEN WHEN YOU GO IN THE MORNING, THE BUYER MAY BE BUSY, OR NOT YET RETURNED FROM SOMEPLACE, SO YOU WILL BE STANDING THERE WAITING. SOMEONE, MAYBE A GIRL CALLED.....

Johanna says, "Come on in." The office is a simple place where odd merchandise is scattered about, where an appointment book lies opened to a page with your name on it, where forms and memos make up the wallpaper and where Johanna is packing boxes on the side. Very unpresumptuous. You may find yourself feeling pretty good sitting there talking with Johanna.

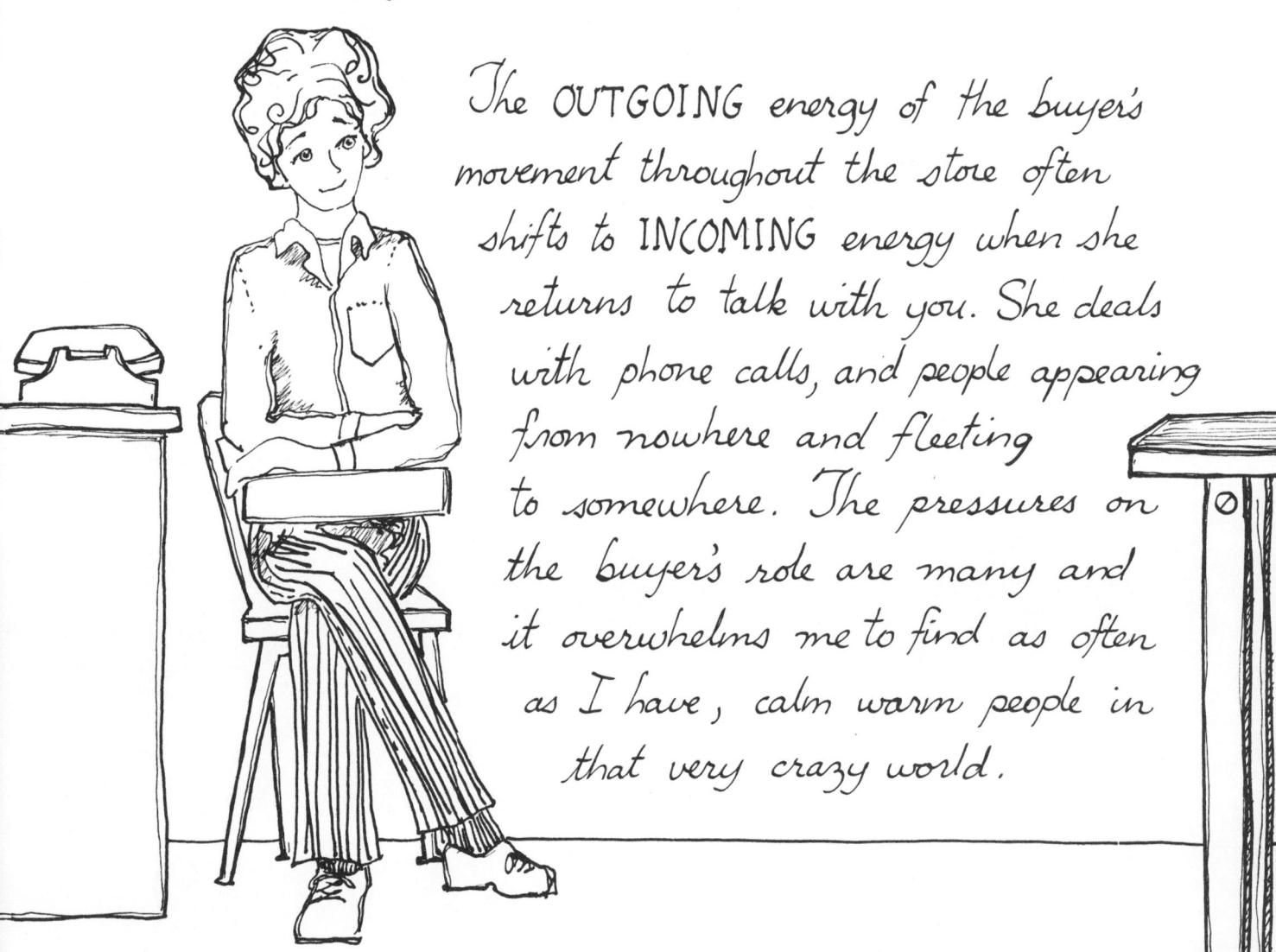

The OUTGOING energy of the buyer's movement throughout the store often shifts to INCOMING energy when she returns to talk with you. She deals with phone calls, and people appearing from nowhere and fleeting to somewhere. The pressures on the buyer's role are many and it overwhelms me to find as often as I have, calm warm people in that very crazy world.

The buyers in big stores discuss your work more frankly than those in little stores. There are the same questions as before (page 37), only more concise and clear, which is all the better for you. Between her knowing what she WANTS and your knowing what you HAVE, clutter is low and the interaction is smooth.

ORDERING...

The ordering is done with a purchase order from the store. This is a form rather absurd in appearance but helpful in effect. Basically it has this information:

1. date of order
2. date to ship
3. cancellation date
4. department no.
5. our order no.
6. terms
7. vendor (that's you)
8. shipping instructions
9. quantity, description, unit cost, total cost
10. buyer's signature

Here's what a typical purchase order looks like ⟶
The buyer fills it out and you are given the original top copy. Remaining is a pile of assorted colored carbon copies that have a profound fate in some super esoteric filing system that you need never touch.

The CANCELLATION DATE is simply a date sometimes set at which point the order is trashed if your work has not arrived. These receiving dates are worked out between you and the buyer. Be able to give some kind of accurate estimate regarding delivery time.

DATE OF ORDER	DATE TO SHIP	CANCELLATION DATE	VENDOR'S COPY
— —	— —	— —	

TERMS OF PAYMENT:
FROM RECEIPT OF INVOICE OR GOODS, WHICHEVER COMES LATER. ON SHIPMENTS RECEIVED ON/OR AFTER THE 25TH OF THE MONTH, TERMS BEGIN AS THE FIRST OF THE FOLLOWING MONTH.

OUR DEPT. NO. | OUR ORDER NO. **MT 121370**

Stacy's

P.O. BOX 0000
SAN FRANCISCO
CALIF. 94102
PHONE- 415-767-2676

TERMS
____ % ____ DAYS

SHIPPING INSTRUCTIONS

VENDOR:
ORDERED FROM _____

ADDRESS _____

CITY & STATE _____ ZIP CODE _____

STYLE NO.	CLASS	GRAND TOTAL QUAN.	DESCRIPTION	UNIT COST	TOTAL COST	SIZES	10	11	12	13	14

BUYER'S SIGNATURE | DATE | TOTAL COST $ | MERCHANDISE ADMINISTRATOR'S SIGNATURE | DATE

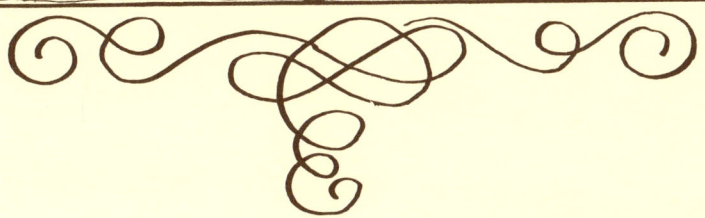

TERMS indicate the method of payment. The most common is called "2/10." This means there is a 2% discount if payment is made by the 10th day of the following month. This statement is often included too: "On shipments received on or after the 25th of the month, terms begin as the first of the following month." In other words, you get paid a month later. Example: Your order is received on April 15th. If the store pays you by the 10th of the following month — May 10th — then the discount is 2%. But if your order is received on April 25th — then the discount is in effect all the way to the 10th of the next month — June 10th.

BATIK

SHIPPING INSTRUCTIONS explain where to send and how to pack the items. They will probably say to pack and label merchandise for each store separately, but to combine these packages into one shipment and mark them with such things as department numbers, order numbers and store numbers. All these numbers, quite fortunately, are clear on the purchase order. A specific carrier is sometimes designated for larger shipments. Otherwise, parcel post is good. Always get a certificate of mailing from the post office. These are general conditions. Shipping ultimately depends on what you and the buyer decide together and often involves nothing more than dropping off a box of goods on your way to get some ice cream.

Sometimes a buyer will request the order to be a SAMPLE ORDER to try in one store, probably the main store. If it sells there, she will purchase for all the stores. Write the words "sample order" on the form you send with the order.

Big store buyers like....

CHANGE

They're always looking for something new and will try just about anything that hasn't been tried before. You can use this to your advantage when arranging a second visit~ which is indeed something you have to initiate. Rarely are there phone calls out of the blue for reorders. Nevertheless, it is no obstacle. All you have to do is call up and explain that you have made this new thing or set of things and that it is...

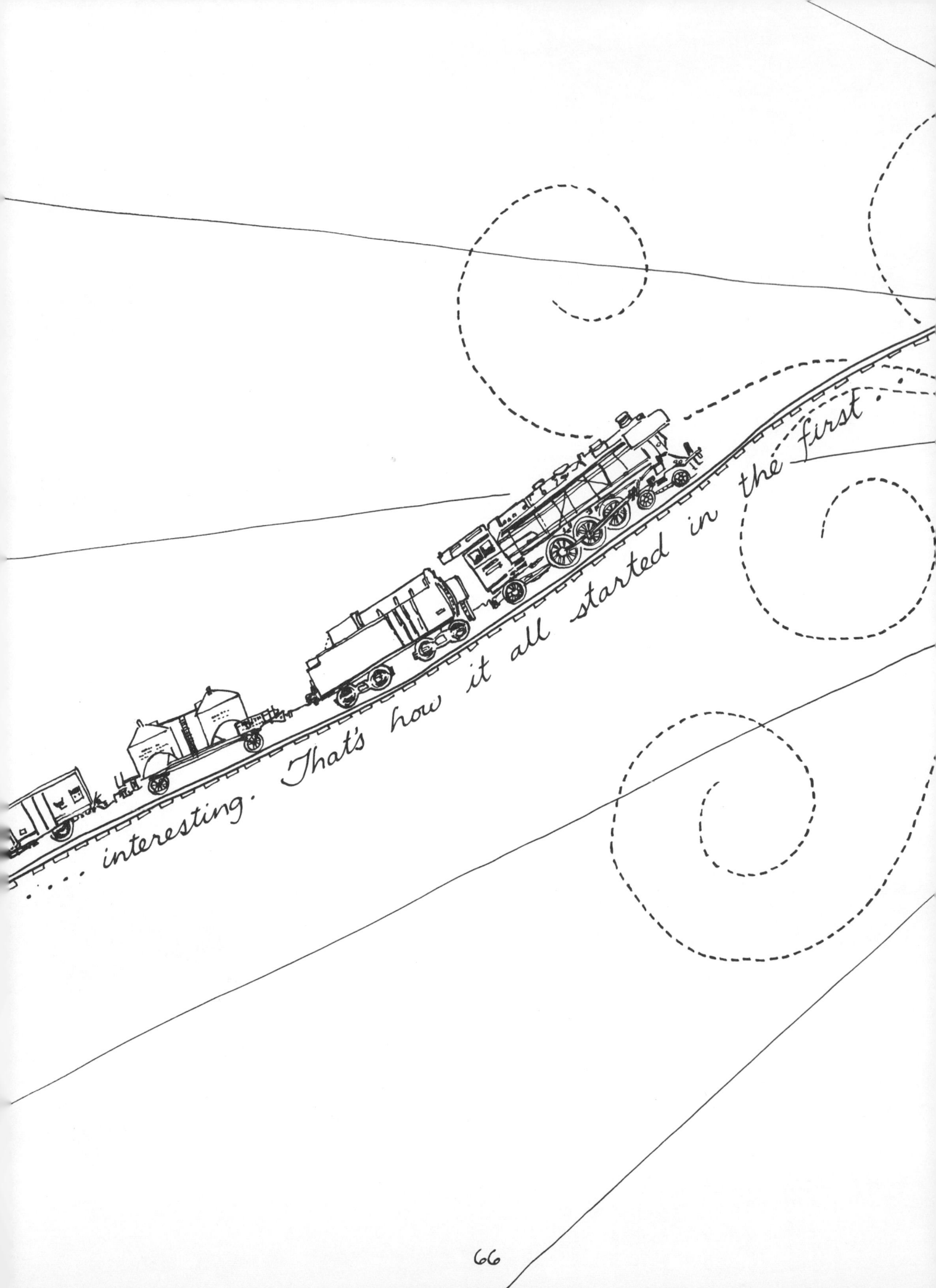

Wholesalers

Wholesalers buy things, then sell them to little and big store buyers. It is very common for wholesalers to buy handcrafted work. Some wholesalers are stationary, some roam about and some do both.

The stationary wholesaler has a showroom where all the items he sells are displayed. A store buyer comes and browses around like a shopper in a store -- except that when it comes time to buy, the quantity is in dozens. The wholesaler writes the order down, sorts what comes from where and sends out the corresponding orders to the makers of the items.

The wholesaler who travels takes the displays to different places, either directly to the store buyer or to buyer's shows around the country. The shows are like artfairs with store buyers wandering around making purchases.

PRICES

Wholesalers usually have a standard mark-up on prices. Arrange it so that you and the wholesaler are giving the same prices to stores because the two sometimes intersect. A buyer who has bought directly from you may come across your work through a wholesaler.

Consider the following three things when making a price for a wholesaler...

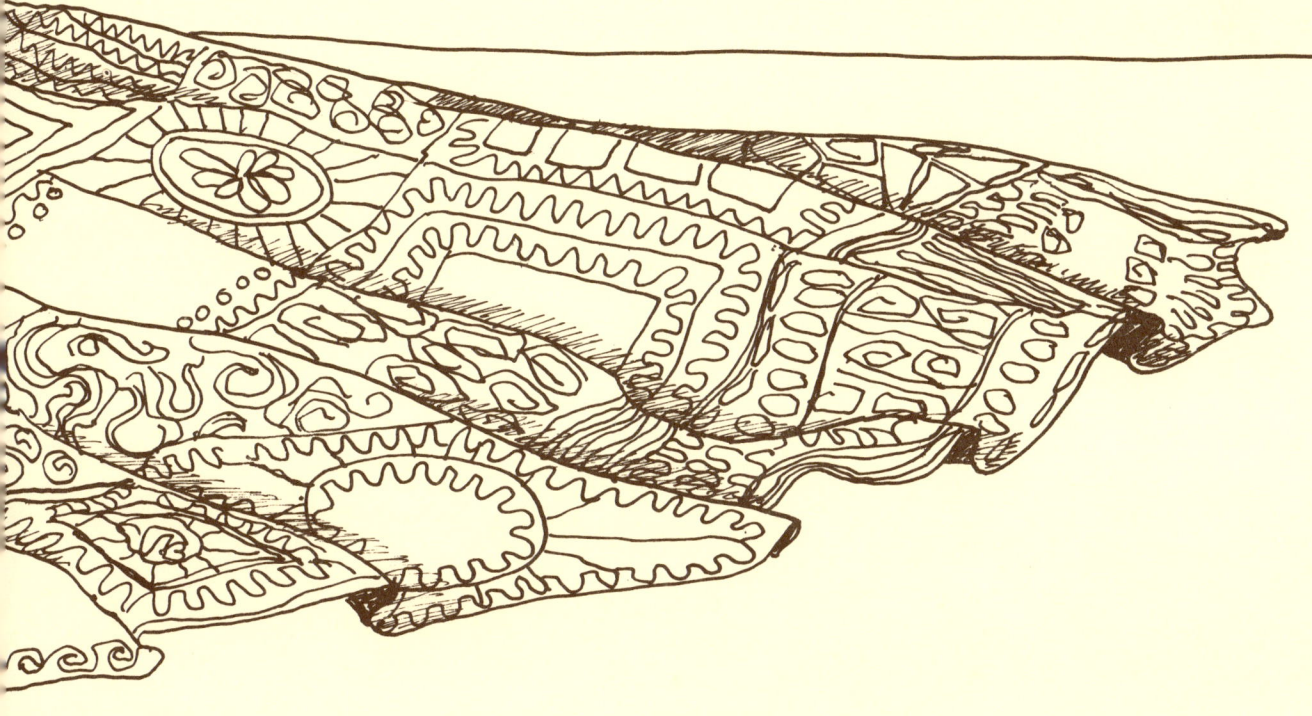

HOW MUCH OF YOUR WORK IS SOLD? If a particular wholesaler sells very little for you – not much more than a regular store – then a lower wholesale price may not make sense. But if there is a considerable movement of your work, then the lower price is justified by the time saved in not having to get orders on your own.

HOW IS THE SHIPPING ARRANGED? Are you responsible for delivering the work to each store or do you deliver to the wholesaler? The order you receive is often an assortment of orders from many stores, so a single delivery to the wholesaler is the cheapest and simplest way for you.

HOW IS THE BILLING ARRANGED?

This is important. Where does the responsibility lie for collecting the money? You can either send a statement once a month to the wholesaler and deal with it as one sum or you can be expected to collect from places possibly all over the country. The latter can be a bad deal unless the wholesaler has accounts to whom he's been selling for quite awhile. When the accounts are known, the risk that may have been passed along to you is replaced by a transfer of trust - a much better deal. The shipping and billing arrangements usually coincide.

The effect these factors have on price varies. Here are two typical situations I have had:

15% AND THE RISK LIES ON YOU

A girl named Jo sells my work. I set up a few displays for her that she can easily carry with her. She takes them to stores and jewelry shows and she has a small wholesale room. The price she gives is the same as I give to stores. She knows her accounts pretty well. When she sends an order, I send the work directly to the store and bill them as well. The responsibility for collecting the money lies on me and for every dollar's worth of work ordered, I give Jo 15 cents in cash.

33% AND THE RISK LIES ON THE WHOLESALER

One time I went to a buyer of a store and he turned out to be a buyer for a chain of stores and a wholesaler as well. He took my work and displays it in a wholesale showroom. When he sends an order the things he wants are separated into groups on the purchase order, each group designated by a six-digit number-name which represents a store that I will never know. The instructions for shipping are to separate the groups and label them with their corresponding six-digit names and send them off in one box to the wholesale company. Then it takes only one bill at the end of the month and a couple of encouraging phone calls ten days later to get the money. The wholesaler keeps 33 cents out of every dollar.

Here are four different trips for a candle that retails for $6.00

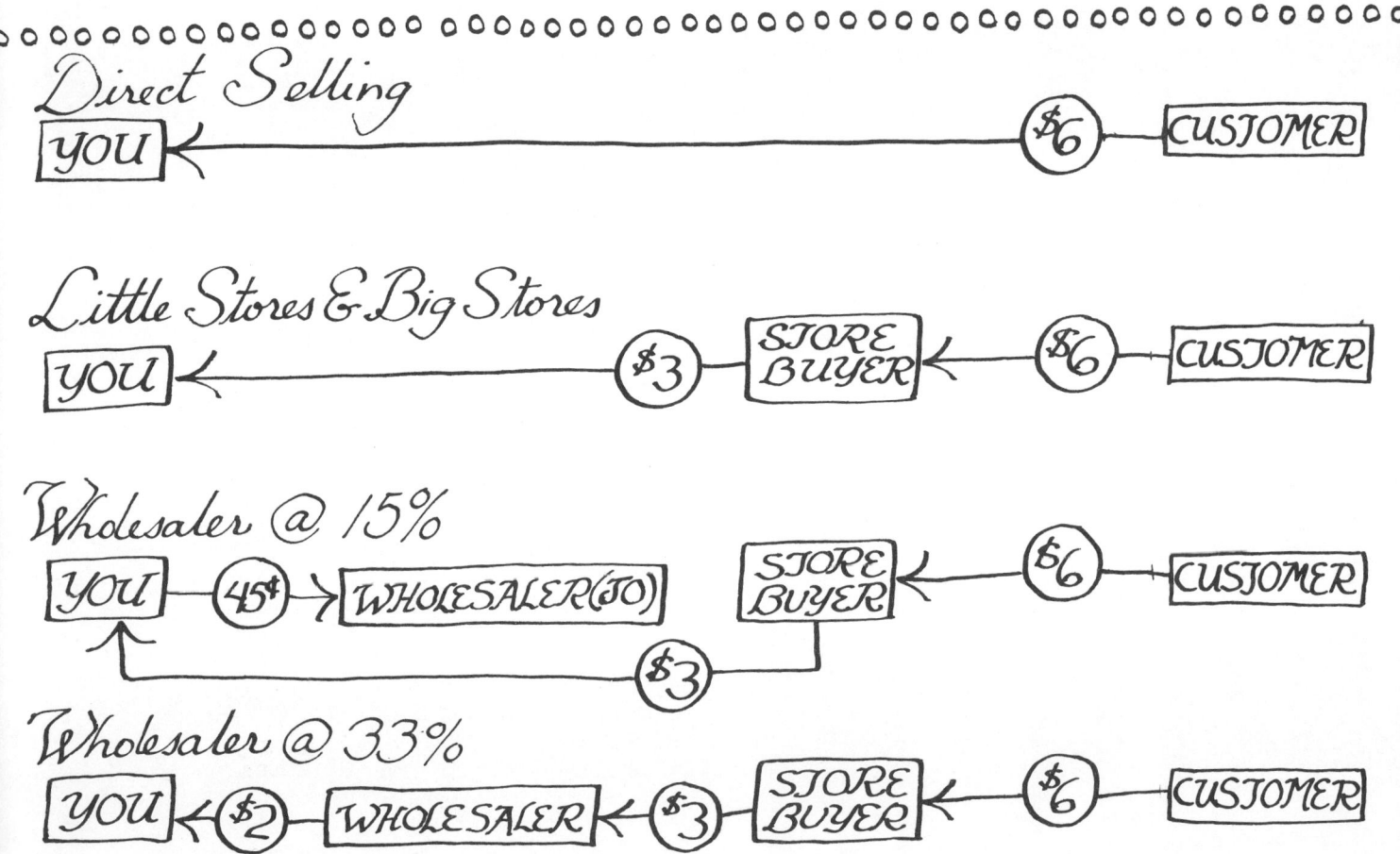

6

You can look at a pile of your own candles or macrame belts and it all makes sense. You designed them, you made them and you've been looking at them for quite some time. You could probably accept quite calmly a whole roomful of whatever it is you make. But think about what it's like to look at something for the first time, like when your uncle shows you his entire stamp collection, when somebody else shows you butterflies, antiques, or pictures of airplanes. It is one crazy thing after another until some time has passed when the chaos can settle within you to make a pattern. However, a buyer does not have as much time to assimilate the patterns in your

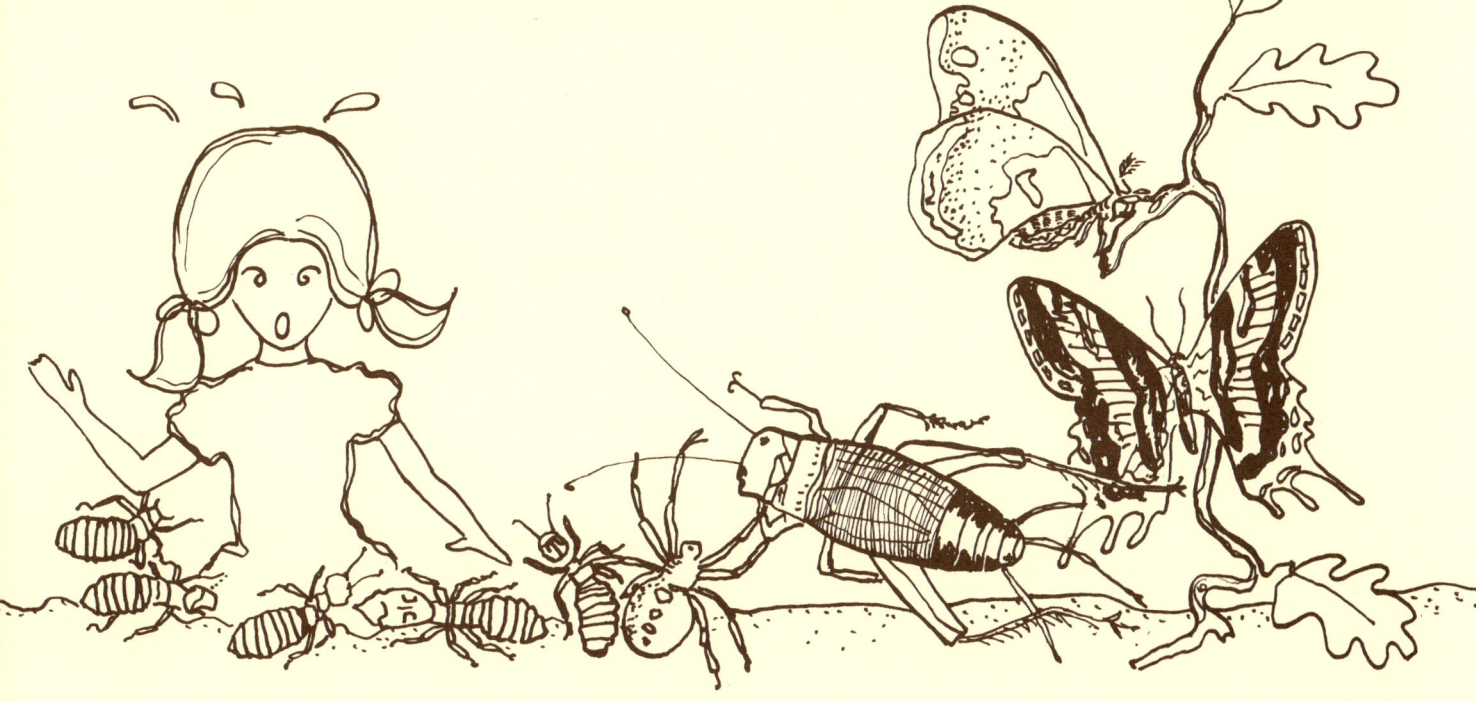

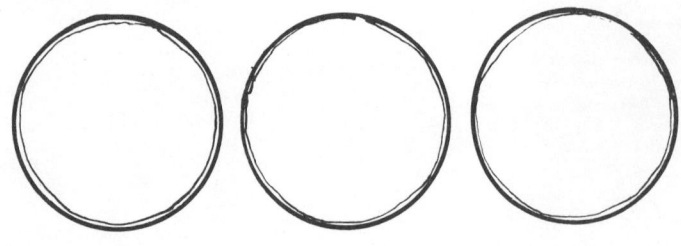

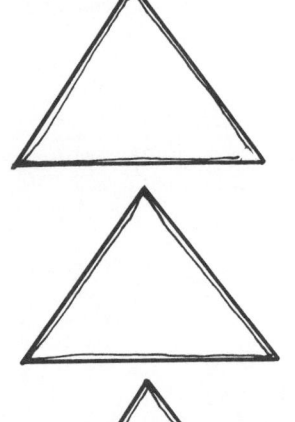

work at the same time she is judging it, pricing it and thinking about calling her cat's vet during lunch break. YOU have to make the pattern, YOU have to make obvious the sense in your work. That's what a presentation is all about.

PRACTICALITY

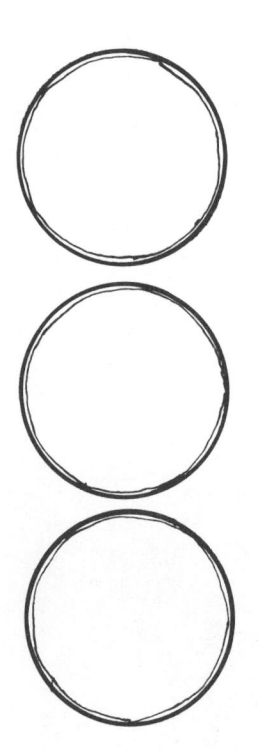

You could put all your little stuff in a sheet, sling it over your shoulder and tow the big stuff around in a wagon but you will have trouble getting up the escalator, let alone through the door. Use something that can be easily carried around. Pictures are good if your work is big stuff. Use something that can be opened and shown smoothly, without a lot of clutter so the buyer won't feel obligated to relieve you of disjointedness by holding a bunch of things. Smoothness is not difficult, clutter is.

It's not so much the number of things that determines smoothness as it is the arrangement, like all the stars in the sky.

The range for the number of items in a balanced presentation is bounded by an upper and a lower limit. The upper boundary is CHAOS. You know you have reached it when the buyer's decision becomes a difficult extraction... zonk... like getting the bug out of your soup. The lower boundary is RIGIDITY. It is reached when there are not enough choices for the buyer to accept some and deny others. Most people need the option for both. If the selection is too small then the only denial option is to deny the whole thing. Between the high and low is a huge space for play.

PATTERNS & BALANCE

Good patterns and balance constitute the aesthetic aspect of a presentation. My friend Hal makes beautiful gold cast rings and he sells them in those high-class, sparkly places. When he first tried selling he went into a store where all the ladies were of fashion in long black dresses. They sparkled like the jewels as they moved behind glass counters filled with diamonds and magic. After finding the lady who was the buyer, Hal stood beneath the crystal chandelier and presented his rings, each one wrapped in green toilet paper and the whole thing wrapped in white diapers. But the ladies saw only the pile of toilet paper and diapers which had grown to a remarkable size and the buyer bought nothing. The work Hal did was incredibly fine and the presentation was practical, but in the eyes of the observers it had no aesthetic patterns or balance.

BACKGROUND

Whether you show the work through pictures or in real life, you can do a lot with background. Jewelry shows well against something dark and deep. Pottery shows well with an earthy background such as a straw mat or a neutral shade. Or try a background with a completely opposite nature from what you are showing. Contrast does wonders. There is contrast in COLOR as in dark vs. light. There is contrast in TEXTURE as in rough vs. smooth, flat vs. deep and on and on. Try different things. A background can compliment your work as well as be practical by holding it together - particularly if you have lots of little stuff.

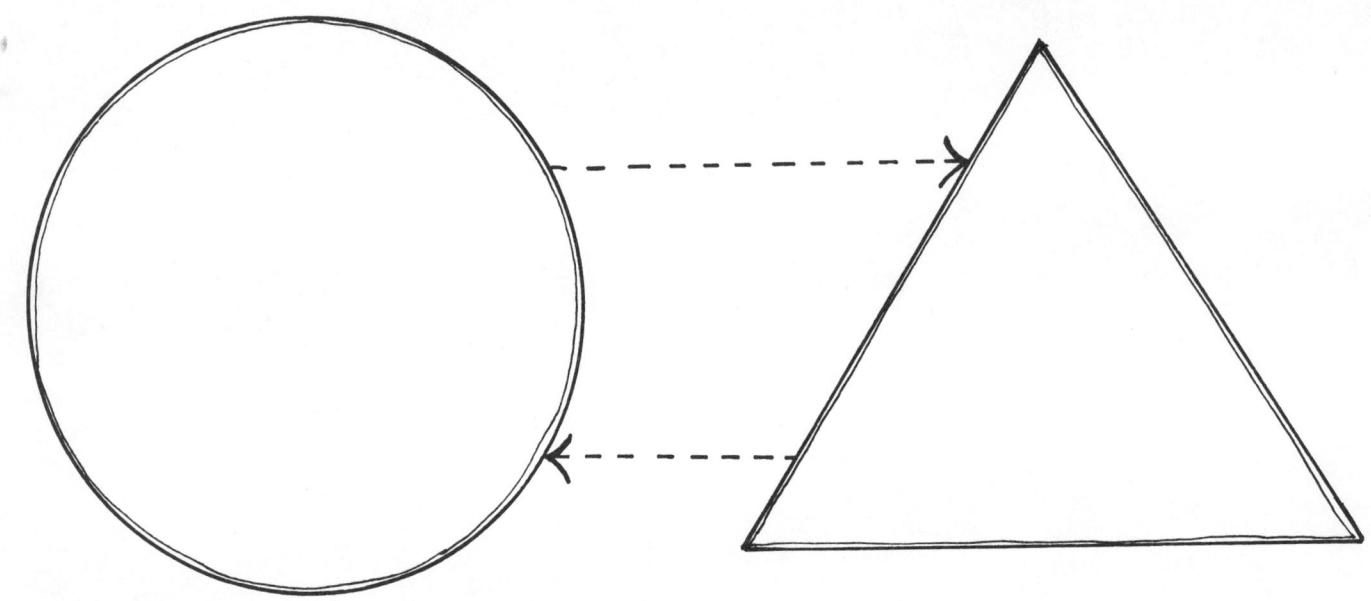

Your presentation should show how the parts of your work relate to each other. This is the pattern part that you want to make obvious. There are so many aspects that can tie things together~shape, color, use, price, material.... When any one of these is connected there is more sense, more comfort in what you have. These patterns are important to the buyer because she in turn will be looking for ways to display.

An Ordering System

The final phase of clarity in a presentation lies in the ordering system. You want a way to write down on paper what the buyer wants. One buyer will simply say, "I'll take an assortment. How about three dozen?" Then you need only remember the number. Another buyer will be more specific. Then you need a way to go from a gesture language -- when the buyer points and says, "Some of this... and some of that..." to a written language -- when the order is put on paper.

The level of the ordering system depends on the patterns that run through your work. Of the different variables possible —— FUNCTION, DESIGN, COLOR, MATERIAL... choose a couple that are strongest in your work. Then separate your work into groups according to these variables.

Here is an example of an ordering system for pottery which could be separated by FUNCTION and COLOR. Separation by function is when you put all the soup bowls in one group and the plates in another. Separation by color is when you put all the green glaze pottery in one group and the purple glaze in another. The intersection of function and color designates a particular item.

Now, give a number and a letter to each separation.

FUNCTION:
plates - P
bowls - B
mugs - M
teapots - T

COLOR:
grey waxy mat glaze - 1
celedon glaze - 2
stoney white glaze - 3

Resulting are notations like this:

    1 doz P-1
    1 doz B-1
    ½ doz T-3

Or how about an ordering system for candles? Well, they all burn, so you can't make separations by function. You can use DESIGN and COLOR....

DESIGN:
- round -   1
- tall & skinny -   2
- square -   3
- cylindrical - 4" - 4
- cylindrical - 7" - 5

COLOR:
- red -   R
- orange - O
- yellow - Y
- green -   G
- blue -   B
- indigo - I
- violet - V

Your notations would look like this:

1 doz   2-R
3 doz   4-B
2 doz   5-R & Y

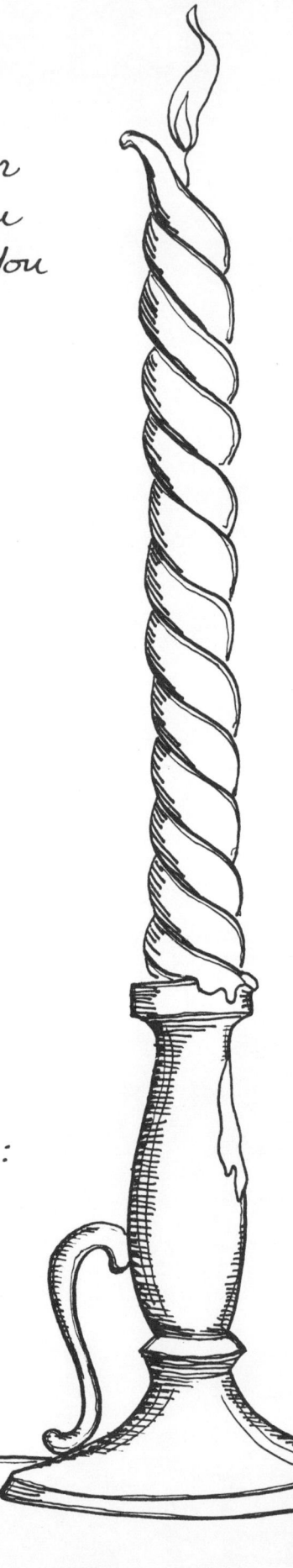

7

FORMS & RECORD KEEPING

The best way to grok a form is to look at one head on. Once you have it in front of you there is just a simple process of filling in the blanks. Most little stores don't care about forms. Big stores and a few scattered ones are into this paper work.

The three forms you will need are:
INVOICES
STATEMENTS
PACKING SLIPS

They appear quite similar but with a closer look you can see their peculiar differences. You can buy these forms at your local office supply store where they sell rubber bands and erasers.

You definitely don't have to go out and have fancy names printed up on the top. For some people this is the first thing they do; for some of these same people it is the last. (Have a rubber stamp made if you want.) Just buy a blank set of invoices, statements and packing slips. The ones that make duplicate copies are best because you will have a record of what you have done.

INVOICES

For every order you send out there is a corresponding invoice. Big stores and wholesalers occasionally request two or more, in which case you should Xerox one and keep your duplicate copy. The invoice tells what you are sending. It is mailed separately from the order. Write "invoice enclosed" on the outside of the envelope. It has these blanks to fill in:

NAME & ADDRESS OF VENDOR – that's you.

OUR NO. – that is the number printed in the corner. If your forms have none you can make one up.

DATE – that's now.

CUSTOMER'S ORDER NO. – use the number on the store purchase order. If there is no purchase order leave it blank.

TERMS – usually 2/10 as explained before.

SHIPPING – (i.e. method) parcel post or whatever you do.

SHIPPED TO – sometimes you ship to one place & mail invoice to another

QUANTITY –
DESCRIPTION –
PRICE –
} relating to what you send. If you are not sending everything that was ordered, write down only what you are sending.

	OUR NUMBER
	6749
	DATE
	CUSTOMER'S ORDER NO.
	TERMS
	SHIPPING

SOLD TO _____

_____

_____

INVOICE

SHIPPED TO _____

ADDRESS _____

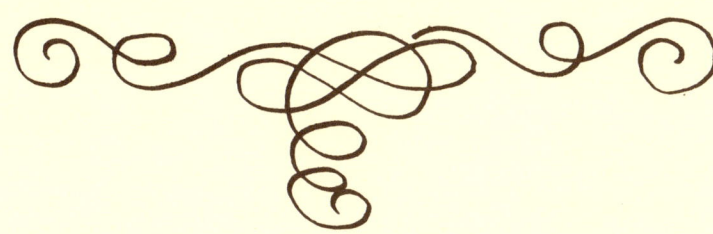

Although little stores usually don't care whether or not you send an invoice, it can be a good way to have a record of what is happening.

PACKING SLIP

A packing slip looks like an invoice except it tells only what is in a particular box and it is sent in that box. For instance, if you send one order in three boxes to Big Store Inc., then send one invoice (separately in an envelope) and three packing slips (one for each box). Packing slips make a way for the people on the receiving end to count and verify what has arrived. Write the invoice no. and the purchase order no. (if there is one) on each packing slip.

STATEMENT

The statement is a bill for what is owed to you. Small stores often pay upon receiving the work, so you need nothing more than a receipt. Otherwise send a statement at the end of the month. If one store owes you for more than one order, include everything on the same statement. Again, write down the corresponding invoice and purchase order numbers.

statement

DATE _____ 19___

TO _____

ADDRESS _____

CITY _____

INVOICE NO.	DESCRIPTION	UNIT COST	TOTAL COST

STATEMENT

RECORD KEEPING

There are some very elaborate bookkeeping systems you can get into, but such complexity is for its own sake. You actually only need to do a couple of things to keep yourself straightened around in terms of what went where and what is coming when or is yet to go there.

I will tell you about two levels of keeping records. I began on the second, then found out the first is all that is necessary. It depends on your situation. Both levels are a cinch.

FIRST LEVEL... *simplest*

Buy your invoices in the book form so that when you send off one, the duplicates remain attached to the book. That way you know what went where. When you receive payment for an order, slash a line with a pen in the upper right-hand corner and write the date. If someone pays you in part, for instance, when the 2% is forgotten, then don't make a slash but note the date and how much was paid. Thus all the invoices with slashes designate orders that have been paid. All the invoices without slashes designate orders not yet paid. At the end of the month when you send out the statements just do the ones that have no slashes. And that is the extent of the first level.

SECOND LEVEL

When a place is buying from you several times a month, the slash method can be confusing because it is unclear what payment corresponds to what invoice. You need a way to keep a running balance that can be easily continued with the movement of any amount of items or money, and one that can be expressed positively or negatively. The standard ACCOUNTS RECEIVABLE method is the best way to keep a record of running balances. "Accounts Receivable" is just somebody's way of saying "the guys who pay you."

Use a separate sheet of paper for each "account receivable." There is special paper you can get at office supply stores with the columns and lines already there or you can do it real country and make your own lines. At the top of each sheet write the name and address of the account (the store). Then make five vertical columns with these headings:

1. DATE
2. INVOICE NO.
3. CREDIT
4. DEBIT
5. BALANCE

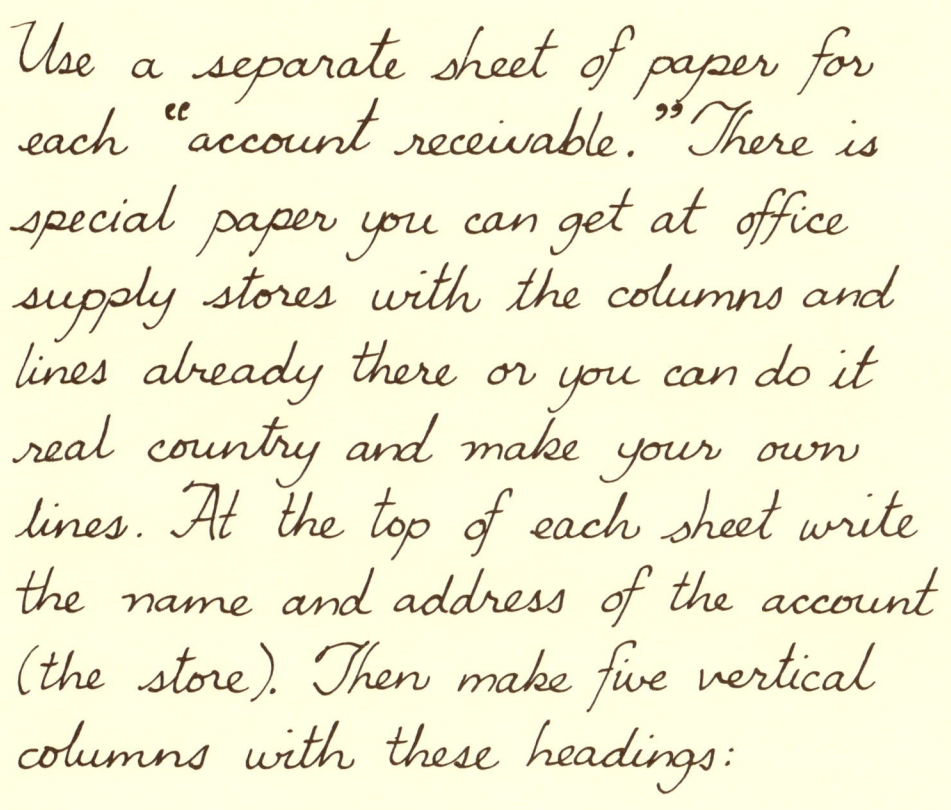

The first two columns are for the date and invoice number. The last three columns are squished over to the right side and contain only money figures.

DATE is the date of the invoice.

INVOICE NO. is the number on the invoice.

CREDIT is an amount of money you receive.

DEBIT is an amount of money owed to you for a particular order of goods sent to the store. Credit and debit are strange words. You could call them "money in" and "money out."

BALANCE is the net amount owed to you.

Here is an example...

You send $27⁰⁰ worth of tubers to B.S.I.
    B.S.I. pays you for the tubers.
You send $30⁰⁰ worth of jissums to B.S.I.
You send $10⁰⁰ worth of biffles to B.S.I.
    B.S.I. pays you for the biffles and the jissums.

Things to note about accounts receivable record keeping:

- A horizontal line in the balance column means no one owes anyone anything.
- The invoice no. for which a store is paying is usually marked on the check, so you know which is for what.
- At any point along the way if you subtract the sum of the credit column from the sum of the debit column you should arrive at the same figure that is in the balance column. This is a good way to double-check if you doubt your own accuracy.

Big Store Inc.
Megalopolis Way
San Francisco, Cal.

Date	Invoice No.	Debit	Credit	Bal.
1/15	no. 1002	27 00		27 00
2/5	no. 1002		27 00	—
2/15	no. 1004	30 00		30 00
2/29	no. 1005	10 00		40 00
3/17	nos. 1004, 1005		40 00	—

Collecting Money

Here are a couple of tips in case you have any trouble collecting money. I have found no cases of acute non-payment but sometimes there are cases of slowness: PROCRASTINATION OF THE PAYMENT.

A normal time span for sending money is any time within the month following the first statement. If you receive nothing in that month then send a second statement with "past due" written boldly upon it. Or if the store is in the area, a phone call is good. Don't get heavy, just ask to speak to someone in accounting. They will probably tell you that your invoice is lost or that they plan to get to it soon. All you really need to do at this point is get the name of the accountant so you will know who to ask for next time.

There is a minor phase of procrastination of the payment which sometimes shows itself quite innocently in the check you receive. You may be so glad to have the money that the fact that 2% was deducted slithers by your perception. The deduction is invalid if the date is past the tenth of the month or whatever was stated in the terms. It may be a mistake on their part, but whatever, you should rebill them for the 2% so that no wishy-washy patterns take root. The 2% might seem small but it'll add up in time, enough that you might buy a pizza pie.

Finally, and rarely, there is CHRONIC PROCRASTINATION OF THE PAYMENT. If the store is in the area and you have made several calls, then go to see the person. Don't make a bunch of threats upon which you will not act. Any store person knows you are not likely to get a lawyer for what is to the store a mediocre amount. If you contact them enough you will get paid. Actually the most extreme operation I ever had to do was after five months when an accountant said it would be just a bit longer, probably the end of the week. I told him that it was all right and that I would wait there in the office as there wasn't much else for me to do that week. So they paid.

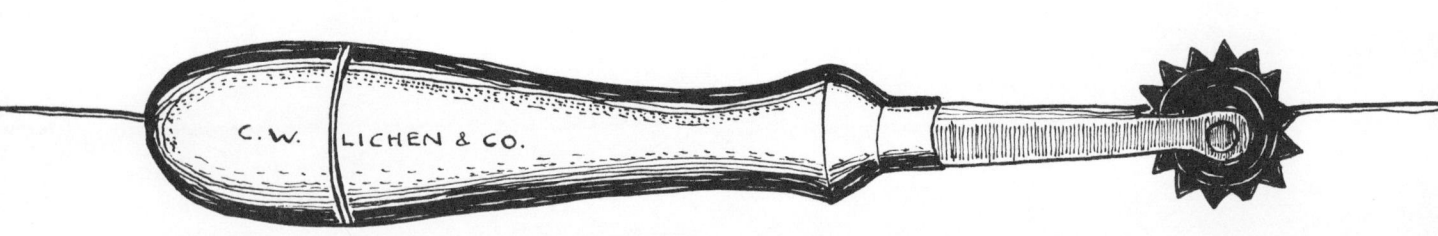

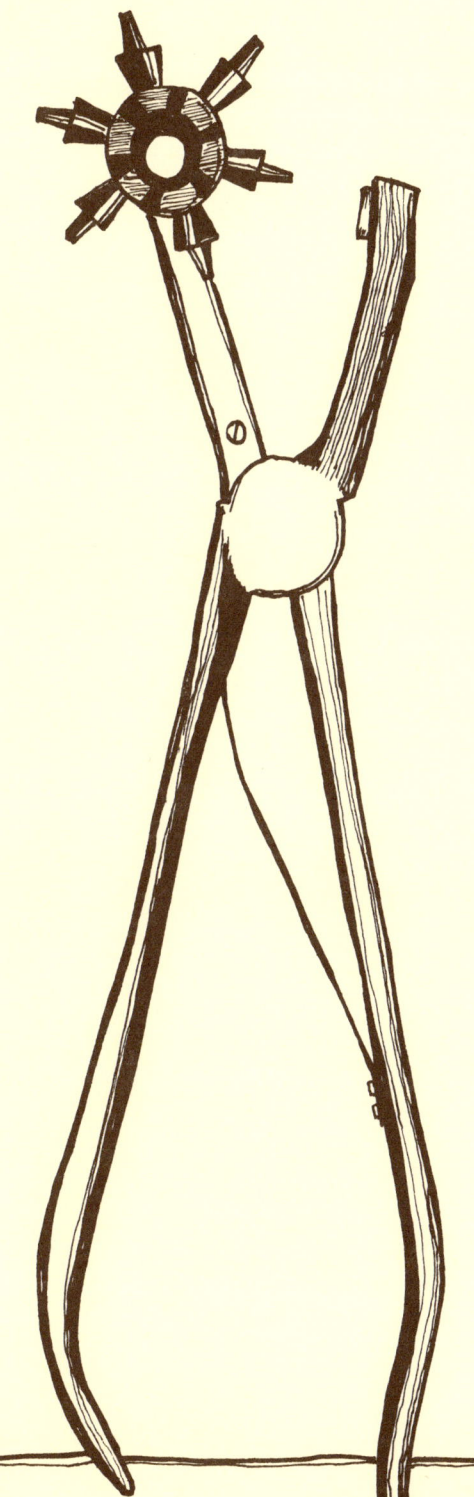

The best way to treat procrastination of the payment is to prevent it. If you are in some far-off city selling your work to shops, have them pay upon delivery. If you plan to <u>send</u> to some far-away places you don't know, prearrange it C.O.D. (cash on delivery) unless they have local credit references that you can check. Seems funny to be on the other end of the credit thing, doesn't it?

Now...
   You have the ingredients to selling what you make. All that remains is subtracting the fantasy that makes you hesitate. Zoom in on what you want. You are an artist. Whatever you make, someone else wants some. Sell it and make some more.

Lots of people helped put the **WOWIE ZOWIE** *into the days that made this book happen....*

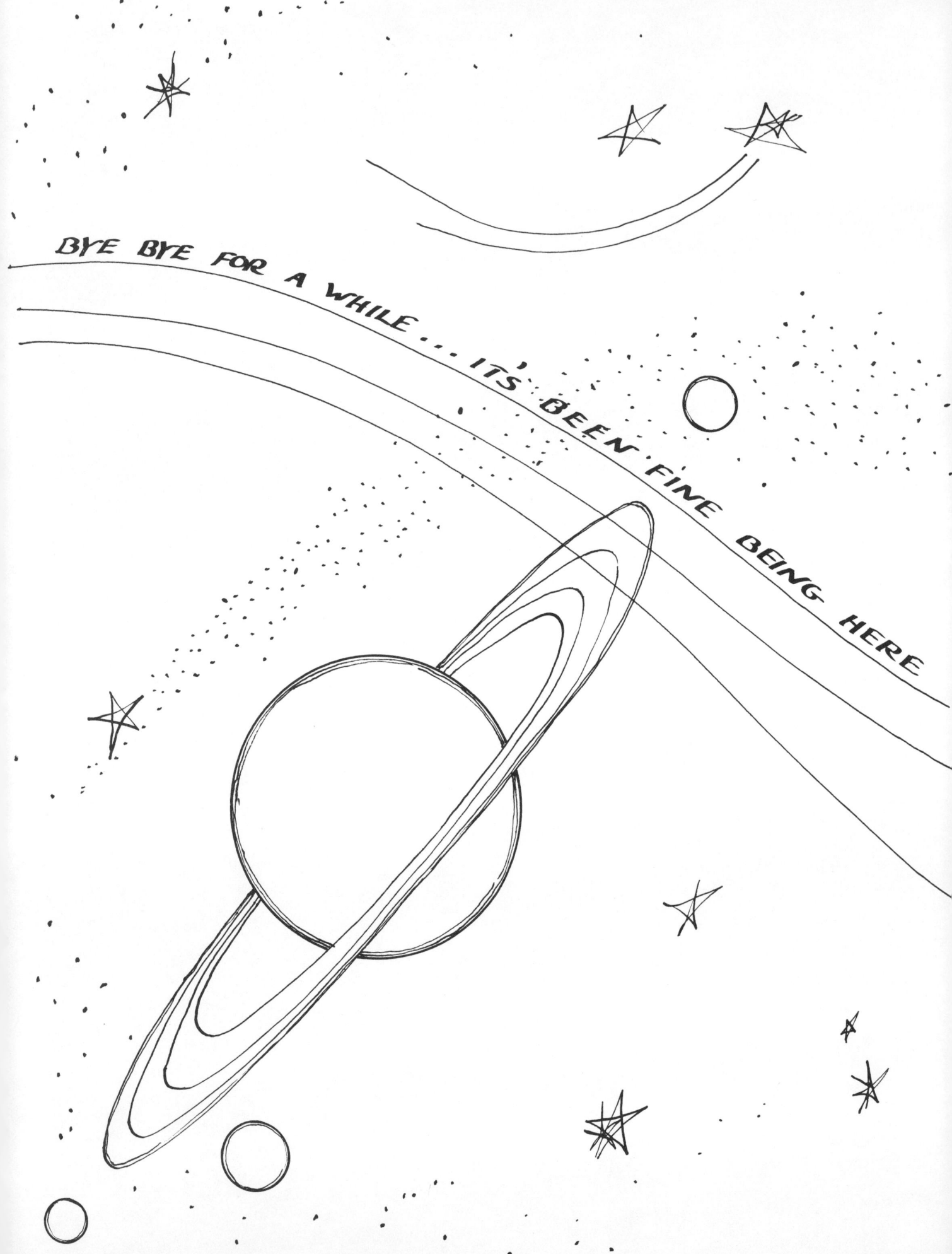